T-MINUS EVERYTHING
~ AND COUNTING ~
THE LEADERSHIP & RELATIONSHIP BOOK

Work Love   Love Work

Shawn Abrams

Copyright © 2020 Shawn Abrams

All rights reserved. No part of this book may be reproduced in any form or by any electronic or mechanical means, including information storage and retrieval systems, without permission in writing from the publisher, except by reviewers, who may quote brief passages in a review.

ISBN: 9798554932052

Printed in the United States of America Published by: Shawn Abrams

www.abrams360media.com

Shawn Abrams

This book is dedicated to the legacies and lives of those we lost in 2020. This has been a hard year, full of surprises and turmoil. This book is my personal response to COVID-19, social unrest, political strife, loss, disappointment, and lack of leadership. I intend to unit people under a new banner. One of hope and purpose.

Special thanks to

Galadriel Grace

Introduction

T-minus Everything and Counting

I know what it feels like to labor, love, and lead people under a closed heaven. No matter how well you try to love them or lead them, no matter how much work you put in, things turn out wrong or worse. Your best-laid plans lie in waste.

I have a desire to help people push beyond barriers to success and purpose. Not everyone will approach these subjects in the manner that I chose, and I respect that.

Now, with respect to my growing audience and possible detractors.

No, this is not your grandfather's leadership book. No, I will not explain complex issues with more complexities. I'm not pushing a get "wealth now" system. There are no shortcuts here. This book is for people who will not go to bed, or the grave, with regrets. I want to teach leaders to teach the people they lead leadership. My hope is that, together, we can help people to become leaders, and help some leaders to become better people.

Yes, I have considered it, it is important, it will work as it was purposed to, I thought it through, and I know the cost. Finally, I prayed, I showed up, and I expect it to work out in my favor.

Why do people need to read a book like this or work with someone like me? Well, we only live in our minds and emotions. And sometimes "we" get in our own way. For those of you who have followed my work, you know I cover leadership and relationships exclusively. Where these powerful aspects of life meet is success, on the way to purpose. And, as life would have it, they zigzag to and fro, coming close enough to each other to bring hope and far away enough to tease hope.

That said, like so many others, I have lost a lot in my life, but I am not a loser. I'm fighting for my share, my history, my legacy, my way, and for those who grow weak in their fight. I write these books, teach, and coach people to do the same. Reader, time may not on our side, but it is not against us either. Time is our enemy only if we fight it. The 'countdown' is a gentle reminder of this. We don't lose confidence; we leave it behind us and find ourselves without it. If you can learn from a problem, you can think like a problem.

If you believe this too, then why not become a problem for your problem? Why not make it a problem for success to evade you? Success is leading failure effectively. This is what we will cover in the following pages. Our success is the path to purpose – that part of the teaching I really enjoy sharing. The relationship we have with people, and the relationship we have with our purposes, which is for people will be explored, and defined here. Remember this: a relationship without definition is a situationship. You will have ample time to consider this and more. It is my belief that when our society lost family, left family, and overlooked family values we lost our important leadership lessons. And, with less people to practice leadership and teach it to others, we all pay the price of inadequate leaders.

The measure of success I have I share with people to live beyond what they perceive as limitations. This is what I want to share with you. It's not a secret or a program. It is a straightforward examination of leadership and relationships; id, ego, and super-ego.

We need to address the "why", which is the universal question – this book will not have all the answers, but it will help us move beyond the need for them. I don't think we need to know all the "whys" in life. The sincere approach to looking for solutions can help us find the how. My teachings stress to ask why in advance of a problem instead of after.

Now, I have found my purpose in pain and problems. Together, they imparted the passion to overcome, succeed, and help others so they too may enjoy a better quality of life for themselves and for those they love and/or lead.

Parts Unknown

In the earlier part of my life, I learned I could understand the problem when I understood the solution. As I matured, I learned I could also understand the problem when I understood the blessing. Now, I know there is a reason, and a purpose, for the problem.

Why do I combine leadership and relationships? Well, whether you love or lead people there should be a relationship in place. Simply leading people doesn't mean that they will follow, and just loving someone doesn't make for a good relationship. I know some of us are or have issues that seem insurmountable, but if these issues didn't kill you, you will have to kill them. If you're reading a book like this and you have a situation like that, then you get to make the choice. I am fond of a graphic that you may have seen. It's a bird that has a frog in its mouth. But the frog is not helpless. His outstretched arms extend to his hands, which are wrapped around the bird's neck. You're in a tight space, but you can make a problem for your problem. For those of you who have read The Seven Epaulettes of Leadership, "This is Beast Mode" was one of the most talked about chapters. I think you will be pleasantly surprised with the next iteration of that mindset – This is Beast Mode, too.

Also included here are "The Relationship Quotient" and "The Leadership Paradox". I'll explain them, tie them into other important themes, and present easy to understand examples.

T-minus everything and counting means time is moving ahead and so is everything along with it. We spend a lot of time counting time – through paychecks, days, seasons, mishaps, traffic lights, etc. Why not count by a controlled system of planning and preparation?

My aim is not to put everything we do in a timeline, but I do want to put what we must do into a structure. It is possible to apply just about anything to a countdown.

The countdown is something we can identify with easily. Recall those times when you were on hold and you said, "If someone doesn't get back to me in ten seconds, beginning now, I'll hang up!" You are committed to this – only, you begin the countdown again. And then, you do another countdown.

That is hope. Nothing wrong with it, but this is not what I want to apply the countdown to.

This may be how some of us approach our goals, with haste, and then regret. I get it, time is important.

Never do a countdown out of impatience, as we will lose sight of what we set out to do in place of marking the passage of time. And, you know what? We never get what we want with the "frustration" countdown. No one worth their vision will build a rocket to attain their comfort zone. Rockets are built to explore and challenge. Now, some people get stuck in their history and in their feelings. You can't put a rocket on top feelings – that's not right. If it's fear and hate the drives you to greater heights, your payload is, essentially, a bomb.

Keep Counting

I remember when eBay started using countdowns on auctions. It made me focus and tune in to them. It was exciting when I wanted to purchase something with just minutes left, but more exciting when I was the seller watching bids come in and time slipping away.

This is why we are using it here. Pay attention to the thing(s) you want to take off in your life. We are on our way to improving the way we lead and love people. This will help us to coach others to do the same. If you live or work with them you would be doing a great service.

The countdown is not what you want to change about yourself as much as what you want to change about your situation.

I received a review for my last book from a woman that did not agree with one of my points – she said as much. But she was so impressed with the rest of the book that she said she would read it with her husband. I think it is great that this couple can continue to talk about relationship matters and read a book together. And, of course, I am flattered that they would read my book together. Even if their responsibilities within the relationship are not equal – they never will be, they chose to lead their relationship, together.

Let me use this fictional couple to introduce another point. In the movie "Mahogany", Billy Dee Williams and Diana Ross play love interests. I will argue that one has a dream and the other has a vision, but I will let you define them. They both have big dreams that eventually materialize in clashes between them. He wants a better life for people in his community and she wants a better life for her. She wants to be a star, and so her motivation, mode of travel, and destination is about her ego. Spoiler Alert: She comes back to him, her true love. The end of the movie is my favorite part – the chemistry between them is still evident. And so, these people, after trying times in their lives overcame their different trajectories, payloads, and launch times to come back together – that was a movie.

Movie endings are only good when they are scripted to be so. How many of us know that real life does not always have nice endings?

The Leadership Paradox

When you lead people, you learn about leadership. And when we teach people, we learn about teaching. I lead and teach every day. Consequently, I can remain well versed and relevant. And, because the circumstances we live in are always changing, we as leaders need to adapt to them, and in some cases change them. I know, we can't change people. But I will show you how change can be done.

Now that I have made this clear, you are forewarned, which is to say, you are forearmed.

These are my words, the words of a man unleashed by circumstance and tempered by it.

And now, without further ado:

T-Minus Everything and Counting

Table of Contents

Chapter 10 – Think Like a Problem

Chapter 9 – Endeavour

Chapter 8 – Preparation: (Ego)ship

Chapter 7 – Quality Control

Chapter 6 – Look Both Ways

Interlude

Chapter 5 – By Design or Default

Chapter 4 – S.T.A.R. (Stop the Arresting Response)

Chapter 3 – This is Beast Mode, too

Chapter 2 – Checkmate

Chapter 1 – Lift Off/Launch

Welcome to the Archives

The Next 5 Minutes with Shawn Abrams

Interview with Abrams

Chapter 10 – Think Like a Problem

A problem is a situation or a condition that you must engage to overcome.

The problems of today will become the triumphs of tomorrow. As they press down on us, they also bring together and compact the things we need to stand where we are. Furthermore, the "shape" that they leave us in is not just suitable for now but also for "next." Later in this book I will share with you how what we go through is not just for us.

Some problems are absolute, and others may seem that way. Problems are an important factor in human existence and societal development. Problem: we needed a way to communicate over great distances. This led to the invention of radio, television, cellphones, meeting apps, etc. Problem: people were dying of various diseases; cures were developed, or were medications that extended the quality of life.

Look at your own life. You had a bad relationship, which you learned from. The result is that you became more discerning and, because of your maturity, you were in the right mindset to meet the right person.

So, if problems can help to shape our lives, then we can think like a problem to reshape our lives and that of others.

Think Like A Problem

You know how some problems seem to have you locked in at every turn? You need to have the determination of a problem. Let's study problems for a moment. They often have a law behind them. They come with a due date or an ultimatum. They may have given warning. They are absolute. They appear and become progressively worse when they say they will. They bring interest and symptoms. They can be defined or they can have no rhyme or reason at all. Covid-19 is an example – a good example. So far, the virus has defied conventional approaches to medical and social treatment. Can you believe people are arguing over to wear or not wear a mask? It is as if this virus studied us, to thwart every avenue to containment and vaccination we could muster.

But how can we use problems to our advantage? First, we must look at what problems do to us.

They make us think, feel, act or in some cases decide not to act. The latter is not desirable for our example. From the leader standpoint, we want to make people do the following:

Feel – you want people to feel you value them. Feeling is like thinking, we are always doing this. You need to supply the commercial of your vision for them. A campaign of success, hope, and happiness will keep them engaging with you instead of just engaged. Your plan based on logic may not make sense to them, even if you order them to do it. Now, if you make them feel important, you make them feel like your plan for your vision is important, you can make them think about how they can support you. You understand, right? We typically feel our way into situations, and then we try to think our way out of them. Take note: The most impactful leaders will draw you in by your feelings.

Think – the most effective way to get people to think about your vision is to make them see how it will benefit them. If you do this right, you bring them into relationship with your vision. When they speak to you to tell you what they think, you take it in and transform it into words they can feel. Always speak to the heart of the matter. Heart decisions are hard to reverse. If you get it right, you won't have to reinforce your messaging as much. Look at politics. If you speak to issues that people feel strongly about you can do almost anything and they will not leave you. They will even go so far as to advance your agenda without new directives. Failure to get this right will leave them open to others cross coaching them. Or, this could lead to people growing apart.

Act – if we get people thinking and feeling a certain way (our way), it will be easier for us to suggest actions. And this is the whole point. In some lost relationships people take actions to maintain it because of their feelings. Some of us have stayed in relationships that we should have left, and some of us have hurt people that we shouldn't have.

Leaders are Teachers, too

The Act part is so critical. The more leadership influence you have the harder it will be for you to get people to act. I don't mean this in a broad sense of the word, like you have five employees, and then you hired another five. I mean, you are getting promoted, and now you have someone to supervise that provides supervision to a team. You want to get everyone in line with the most senior leadership in your organization. In the Seven Epaulettes of Leadership, I called this the Continuity of Leadership. I want to expound on that theme. You need a customer, client, or constituent to take some action, (let's call them the actor), but there are multiple levels to separate from you.

In order for us to reach the actor and motivate them to take action, we start with the level closet to us. We will teach them the Feel Think Act model and teach them how to teach it to their direct reports. The key here is, I must know how to teach, and know how teach others to do the same. Note: this is not a once-a-quarter training; it is as often as your work, actor, and chain needs it. I know when this process doesn't work, because the customer (actor) doesn't act. I cannot blame the actor, or anyone else in the chain, because I own the entire chain, not just the relationship to the people that are direct reports to me. Now we see that teaching is as important as leading. You need not be an expert teacher. Just base what you teach on the Feel Think Act model. Getting people to feel what you intend to teach is more than half the work.

Now, we as leaders must be mindful of others who try to influence us the same way – against us. This is their strategy. I used that word intentionally, because when we employ Feel Think Act it is for the purpose of achieving purpose. Until we can determine the motives of others, we must assume that they mean to enable us for their use. We must push through our feelings and think about what they want for us, before we act.

We Should See It Coming

We think in images and we recall experiences based on images as well. So, when we share our vision, we get people to feel, think, and act based on the images of our vision. The narrative that we use to support the vision is used to persuade people to act. We must see a thing before we act on it. You saw yourself marrying your spouse, you saw yourself working for that company, you saw what some politician described what life would be like once they are elected to office.

NEXT

One of my favorite questions to ask people is, "what's next?" Maybe they just landed a job great! That's not purpose, that's success – what's next? How do you ensure you have success on your new job? There is always a next

Next is how I can get people to fall into the feel, think, and act structure. Next as a matter of course leads people to act but combine that with a narrative that will make them feel and think will create the path to do this. I have even decided to ask myself the same question. And so, a sampling of my "next" will show up later in this book.

Leading and Teaching

True, we must teach our people to recognize, respect, accept, challenge, administer to, and/or live with a problem. Not everyone is adept at dealing with problems. Someone on our team may have a difficult time with their problems, which in turn could make them appear to be the problem.

Don't make people the problem. Make the problem the problem.

People can be coached to resolve problems. This approach to Applied Leadership raises new leaders, and it makes them bigger than the problem. You would be wise to study counseling, mental health, problem solving techniques, and leadership. Keep contacts to social programs and supports at your fingertips also. Don't assume that because you are a leader you need to be able to resolve every issue your people encounter. We must know when to refer or defer to a quality professional for the well being of those we serve. When you committed to leading you committed to teaching.

I define leadership as a discipline for you, the leader. And so, teaching people leadership is one, teaching the subject matter. And two, teaching them about "you" too as the subject.

Leadership is uniquely you. Ego is the enemy of your leadership. Applied Leadership is the method you employ to lead people; it has two practice areas: coaching and mentoring. Success is a series of steps along the way to purpose. Purpose is given to you. Vision is how you see purpose and how you describe it to others. Personal relationships are not equal; someone will lead by design or default.

Ask Good Questions

Don't ask them if they are upset or why they are upset! They will tell you they are not upset but have actions or even silence that will show otherwise. By asking such a question at a sensitive time that has an obvious answer you run the risk of losing credibility with them. Instead, ask them how they feel. This is where their true feelings will come out. Now you can determine if the situation is within your purview or must be outsourced. So important for new leaders as they often try to "save the world".

They don't make problems like they used to, but that's okay, because they don't make people like they used to either. Take the U.S. Navy S.E.A.L's – honorable men. They take to the water and make themselves comfortable there. They cannot make the water comfortable for themselves. That task would be even beyond their incredible capabilities. But what makes them so special is that they don't just become comfortable in the water, they survive and, most importantly, they thrive in that element. That is, they complete their missions. We can learn from them. Sure, they are a special breed of human being, but they were not born this way. They had to be conditioned to carry out great exploits, to overcome problems, and to win.

This is exactly what we should be training in business. We need to learn problems: how they come about, how to face them, how to overcome them, and how to teach others to do this.

The Problem with Problems

Problems are like objects in the vacuum of space – they all have gravity. If they have mass, they have gravity. For our lives, the "gravity" of one problem seems to attract another problem. They may not combine but they can orbit each other and you too. You have heard it said that problems come in threes, right? That's where I'm going with this. As problems come together, we don't split our resources and face each front. I look for opportunities to combine problems and try to provide one solution.

Example: I have a limited about of time to use a limited about of staff to accomplish multiple goals.

1. I explained to my team that I had a bright vision of our future. I used information they shared with me, individually and collectively to flesh out that vision. I said, "Success is not something we are after. We already have it, but we stand to lose it." (Feeling)

2.   They had very different job functions, but I explained I had a plan that could unite us in spirit and effort so we could all make our respective part successful.

3.   Rather than speak to each person about their individual part, I put the entire plan to the whole team. This was good since everyone offered suggestions, even for work that was outside their sphere of influence. Soon, they volunteered to extend themselves to help the other person. They found unique ways to push us through. The synergy started in that meeting, long before the actual work began. (Thinking and Acting)

Example: I have multiple stakeholders to report to. A few of them needed different metrics. I was able to reduce the amount of work by combing some of the information needed. As a result, some parties received their report much earlier than requested, as I sent most of the reports out on the same day.

Example: I lead and teach my team the way I want them to lead and teach our constituents. It's twofold – no need to set aside a different training for either part, as I consider both parts one team anyway.

The Problem with Leadership

I once spoke to a group of African American youth about the topics we all face as a nation and as a community of color. I acknowledged that African Americans, particularly men, have had deadly encounters with the police. My objective was to say that if a police officer stops you its because you look like a situation to them. This can be true for anyone. Granted, there are some bad officers that will profile for unlawful reasons, but they still see a situation to be investigated, even if we have done nothing wrong. I suggested to the youth that we respond with respect and try to bring humanity into the situation, rather than a combative or avoidance response. I say this in general, and do not mean to imply that this course of action could prevail in every case. Nor do not I say that those who lost their lives to the police would be alive today if they did this. I simply want to find ways for people who encounter this to stay alive to tell their story, instead of some bystander's postmortem account.

Someone in the audience said they were unfairly targeted by the police. He went on to say you can't blame people for pulling away or even running away from rogue officers. I paraphrased his statement. I agreed that if you are unfairly, physically attacked by the police, you have a problem. But non-compliance will only make it worse. Self-preservation should be your top priority. The constitution, civil rights laws, or any set of legally ratified documents lack the density to repel a bullet. The audience member went on to say that the system was not designed for black people. I have heard this before, and I didn't debate it with him, but I did tell him that the "system" is what brought me to talk to the group that day.

The "system" that so many people of color talk about is a mindset, and so many people who feel oppressed by it involuntarily support it by letting all we think about it determine what we can and cannot do. Pay close attention to what I share next. If you feel oppressed and suppressed, and you think the "system" will prevent you from your purpose, and as a result you take no action towards your purpose, you have a problem. But all is not lost, because you have also reverse-learned Objective Purpose.

"Purpose" purpose comes from the creator. Objective Purpose comes from us. My creator purposed me to teach others. My Objective Purpose is to incorporate the things I like into my teaching. You will see that I like dry humor and science – hence my objective purpose. But what we see when some complain about the system is the reverse of the application. Far from the life we need – it is a hindering. Look, if the "system" pre-dates us, and we know what it is, we should study it. And we should use it for our advantage. Take note: a screwdriver wasn't designed to open a can of paint, but we use it for that purpose! It's too easy for some to say that another's outdated mindset is the cause for their lack of motivation or application.

Disappointment will come when looking for equality, which is a 1:1 ratio, or a perfect balance. There is no such thing in nature, or in man for that matter. Your left hand is larger than your right, one of your eyes is larger than the other, your heart is more to the left side of your chest, etc. Now, look at the life of someone who has lost time to equality thinking. They didn't run down the rabbit hole headlong, they backed into it intentionally. Waiting is not the answer, just weighing in is not the answer, but wading in – this is the evidence of our resolve, and the first steps to a banner life for us and contribution to a banner life for others.

I've worked in community-based organizations, funded by the system, which are designed to assist people of color with employment, trainings, education, financial literacy, and social services. I have seen people make use of these supports to improve their quality of life, but not as many as I would like to see. That same day I referred to earlier, we expect a few dozen youth, but only a handful came out. The same audience member complained that people who were invited were home but asleep. I may lose some support here, but I am a black man who has lived in man predominately black neighborhoods.

I shared with the group that police over-policing our black communities is not the only problem black people face. There was a time when black communities policed themselves. I don't mean in the literal sense, I mean in the moral, ethical, sense. Adults had authority and could exercise it over any child. Today, the problem is that people don't recognize authority, and those same people may also struggle with submitting to leadership. Everyone is leading themselves. The presence of national leadership does not make it to every community. Sure, there are ads for election, and there are social programs, but when was the last time you saw someone running for a high office speaking from a public housing development?

I have a church at home and many pastors outside of my church who want me to take part in their services. You see how there is division? Pastors are competing for congregants. We don't need more churches; we need more people to attend the ones that are open – my opinion. Historically, leadership in the African American community stemmed from places of worship. It seems to me that the community has moved away from that. Now, people opt to show support, again, which is important, but force has dissipated over time – it cannot sustain itself. And so, unfortunately, because we resolve to solve these issues with force, we continue the use of it.

Protesting is a show of force, not a show of power. If power were displayed even one time, it would not be needed again. Sure, when force is applied people take notice, but when force moves away a vacuum moves in. Leadership should be the one thing that can transcend church and state, because it is critical to our society.

We should work with our team to define what leadership means, and then explain the kind of leadership that we bring. Ask them what kind of leadership style they subscribe to and work with them to express or develop it. They will get some awesome training and they will understand you better.

The problem with leadership is this: collectively, we don't know how to lead and how to follow. This is not a slight. It is evident that those who are powerful, popular, forceful, resourceful, and perhaps ruthless become leaders. This does not mean nice people cannot lead, but kindness is often taken for weakness.

Problems led to the pursuit and production of energy – great! But energy led to problems with global warming. I'm sure solutions will come, but I'm also sure more problems will follow.

The Problem Approach

The Problem with Relationships

If you lead or love people you can't say that your established position in their lives is enough to weather a storm. Okay, you came around, you see the error of your ways. But sometimes trying to love the one you're with too late is still too late. You want to make your significant other feel, think, and act for you and the relationship. Make it a problem for them to leave you. Make it a problem for them to deny you.

Consider this: medical professionals are trained to learn how the mind and body function, and then they learn about addressing common maladies. The purpose for these two very different trains of thought is to heal. Now, in business we are taught and expected to achieve success. When failure of setback plagues us we are unprepared and sometimes ill suited to offer correction. Subsequently, more time is spent trying to figure out what went wrong versus the entire time of the endeavor.

For success and purpose and objective purpose, we must embrace the Problem Approach.

There are four types of problems for this train of thought:

Constant

You remain the same and you force others to change by virtue of the situation you put them in. And you do this by constantly changing the situation you put them in. At some point they must change. You exhaust them and their resources, forcing them to adapt to a new norm. This is that sink or swim situation some leaders put their subordinates through. It's like hazing – what if they sink? Can you save the assigned task? What about the damaged person's confidence? What about your relationship with them?

*Requires a lot of resources

Changing

You change and adapt solely to keep the other person locked in place. The Corona virus mutated in order to keep us in a state of dis-ease and disease. Or you don't want your spouse to get complacent in the relationship, and so you try to do new and exciting things. Mutating in the latter sense of the word is good.

*Requires a lot of planning and patience

Terminal

This is a seek and destroy mission. You will risk it all by destroying everything they have and everything you have. Once you begin this course of action there is no turning back. They will destroy your reputation even if it destroys theirs

*Requires a death wish (crossing the Rubicon); the die is cast

Irreversible

Just under Terminal in severity but more costly in terms of maintenance. You do not want to destroy them, but you want to make them feel that way, forever. This will become a lifestyle for you. And definitely a form of control.

*Requires all the other problem mindsets

You may be able to escape a problem, but you would cheat yourself out of the lessons you would learn from resolving them. It is generally believed there are four types of problems. If your ego is the problem, when you get to that new place your ego will try to occupy the entire space. Take from each definition to make yourself a problem.

The Problem with Trauma

The only thing that passes through all trauma without treatment is time. Time will continue, we get physically older, but emotionally we can stay at the traumatic event. There is a danger here, if we hold on to that emotional hurt, without properly addressing it, and we continue to grow. We get the degree, we get the marriage, the home, the promotion, and the trauma remains. It may not cause us to lose anything listed here, but it could cause us to struggle with them. Leadership training would not offer a solution, but it can bring to light the contrasts of our actions and behavior as a result of trauma.

Trauma is not something to be ashamed or avoid. Take care of anything that can become a bigger problem later on. Remember, the first person you lead is you yourself.

What's the Problem?

Problems don't panic. They have confidence and dignity, even up to the point when they are resolved. If they could talk, they would say, "it's not personal, this is my function."

Problems:

- Project their power from the time it is detected through the time you gain understanding of it, to the point that it has achieved its end.

- Are intentional – there must be an outcome whether you accept it or not.

- Have authority – they have a right to exist in our lives by law or by nature.

Problems do not lash out in frustration or rage as this may spoil their own position. Once the problem's plan is put into place the work is done. This is a no-maintenance endeavor. And, yes, problems come with countdowns.

The best thing about problems is that they are logical. If they are one kind of problem, they don't become something else. However, they can become a different class of problem, moving to a higher degree of difficulty to resolve.

Problems have gravity too. You rarely get just one by itself. If you have galvanized pipes you have a problem in the making. If you hear water running at your water main and no one is using the water in the house, you're at t-minus some amount of time. At t-minus zero, the problem (water from the city) is coming into your basement. Now you need a plumber to go into a small hole in the ground wearing a wet suit (his problem) and put a special fitting on the pipe to control the water (also his problem), and you don't get off the hook here because the city will give you an official-looking letter that states, "If you don't fix this within forty-eight hours you are going to pay a fine (that's another problem). The plumber fixes that problem, which is good, but now you have to pay an amount that looks like the city fine.

People with these problems look down on others with lesser problems. They say, "Please, I would love to have your little problems." Apparently, they have the Hamptons of problems.

This is an exclusive club. "Regular" people don't have the means to attract problems of this magnitude.

Okay, let the exclusive people sort out their problems.

Moving to the end of the problem is itself a problem, as this sometimes requires us to make changes. Human beings are not like viruses, which naturally mutate as a part of their lifestyle. No, we ignore our problems and hope they mutate to a state more advantageous for us, thereby bringing a their end closer and thus mitigating its effects.

If you follow my work you have heard me say, "Gentle reminder: Don't make people the problem. Make the problem the problem. People can be coached to resolve problems. This approach to Applied Leadership raises new leaders, and it makes them bigger than the problem."

Let me add to that: if you make people a problem you continue having that same problem, because you cannot change people. And few people will want you to change them. I teach leaders to first coach, and then mentor people. Coaching builds people up where they are, and mentoring brings them to where you are. Let's go beyond that. Coaching is how you get to know people and mentoring is how they get to know you.

The sum total of our lives is not your feelings, although it can seem like that.

This is important because some people have a lot of influence over our emotions, which gives them passage to affect our lives. If someone becomes a part of your life for an emotional reason, it would be hard to let them leave – even if they are physically not in our lives.

I had this thing I did with the largest team I had the honor of leading. I would hold that I would ask for a volunteer. Now, half the time the thing I wanted them to volunteer for was beneficial to them – it wasn't even work! It was something cooler and fun. The other fifty percent of the time, it was work, but there was a reward attached to an actor, so there was always a benefit. But no matter how many times I did this, no one ever really just jumped up and said, "I volunteer". Maybe it's the word or maybe it's the unknown, but it tells me that work is not going to move

Leadership is not perfection. Yes, leaders make mistakes. It is okay to share with your team what went wrong. It's okay to let them know that you are human. While running a community-based organization, I once shared that I pay child support. I explained that non-custodial parents may have different situations, but we all have the same responsibilities.

The People v. Your Leadership

So, in the Seven Epaulettes of Leadership, I shared that Leadership is a discipline for the leader – it is uniquely you. You can sit in the same leadership class as someone else and not be the leader they are. Your leadership is on trial every day. That is, your efforts and outcomes are being evaluated constantly. Don't make the mistake of delegating your "evaluation" on to your subordinates. This message is so important. There will come times when you must defend yourself without being defensive.

Perspective

You have this vision for your team to pursue. But to get there, your team needs resources, trainings, leadership, coaching, mentoring, and a vision of their own that fits into your vision. This is so important, as their vision gives them something to own. You don't want them to own a "goal". You want them to own the vision they hold of attaining their goal. To force them to achieve your vision gives them franchisee responsibility with hourly wage pay. It's too much to ask of someone who has dreams and aspirations of their own. Give them equity in the endeavor. Help them develop their vision based on your vision. Now they are working towards what they see and what you see. What they work on day-to-day, which is theirs, will bring them the confidence and success needed to land in your vision.

Don't lead what you want, lead what the team needs!

I wish all leaders understood that teams operate in a three-dimensional plane, but instead they follow a one-dimensional plan that is read left to right top to bottom. Due to the 3D workspace, we need to give people time and space to operate – to recoil. What does this mean? Take a careful look at what you ask your team to do. Everything that sounds good is not always good.

How does what we propose to take on affect what we're already doing?

How will the team receive this new initiative? I've said this before, not even a good plan will work if the people don't feel good about it, or you.

Are we adding new meetings, new reports? Is there collaboration across departments? Do the contact people know each other?

I'm a believer that things just don't work out. You may have to shepherd every process outlined above yourself. Yes, have a meeting, have a call, but it's not about the work; it is about the people who will have to do this work. General formalities aside, I need to know that everyone has "bought in". I need to know where they perceive struggle and success. I could show them how their contribution can do a wonderful thing for the organization, but that is not attractive to everyone. I could tell them how their respective strengths can support each other. I can tell them what they stand to gain. I could ask them what their vision is, in terms of growth, career, and growing others. This way, if the plan needs more pieces or support in unknown areas, they will take care of that without being told. Doesn't it feel good when someone says, "I saw this shortcoming that had to be addressed, and so I took care of it real-time"?

People may know what you're going through, but they don't understand what you're going through.

They see you working and struggling, but they may not understand the struggle because they can't see your vision. Ah, this is a different situation. We may have thought they didn't care – in all the world I'm sure someone has that problem. But I want to ask you how effective you have been with sharing and explaining your vision to your team. Are you clear? Are you intentional? Are you seeing something realistic? Is your vision lining up with that of your boss? Did you help direct reports with their own vision? People will stand there and watch you work. They will stand there and chat you up, ignoring your overtures for assistance because they are not comfortable with your vision or the fact that they don't know what it is. If you have a relationship with this person, you grow them where they are with coaching, and bring them to where you are with mentoring. I find it hard to believe they would not be working with you side-by-side.

How do we teach leadership? Through feeling, thinking, and actions. I find this method the best to get people to not only act, but to remember. And when they have success, they would be more inclined to pass on what they learned. I like to give people the opportunity to teach or facilitate. If this comes naturally for them, even better. We all want our meetings and calls to be lively with participants sharing. I've found that those who contribute generally follow-though on what they suggested. I might even reach out to someone who has a key part of the initiative in advance of a larger meeting to informally prep them. It's the whole coaching thing – you can't get away from it. Applied Leadership raises leaders and teaches them to win. In this case, I describe a win as that continuity line from me to them to the objective.

We don't make the trophy we take it!

Chapter 9 – Endeavor

"Youth is wasted on the young." -George Bernard Shaw

Chinese proverb, "The best time to plant a tree was twenty years ago. The second-best time is now."

I think the later part of this proverb is the realization that an opportunity was lost. And so, the "second-best" time is the second chance.

We all have a shelf life. So why shelve our lives? If you find it too hard to get yourself going, you are not leading yourself. There is nothing like a vision and a plan to get you up in the morning, and for some of us morning is three times a day. Get up early and work that plan!

In life you need a plan for two reasons:

1. Your plan will lead you to a goal.

2. You can use that plan to gauge where you are right now, today, to determine if you have what you need.

You know what happens when you don't have a plan?

You will meet some cute person and they will have a plan for you. This is nice of them, but no one will come up with a plan for your life that does not benefit them. Think about the last time some cute person told you what you should be doing – it did not work out, right?

You see, on the other side of someone else's plan for us is usually disappointment. We're left with the consequences of their plan. That doesn't even sound right – their plan, our life! If we have our own plan, we can gauge what they propose. You might say, "It's nice that you have a plan for my life, and I think it's cute that you included yourself in the plan, but your plan doesn't get me to my purpose."

Most of us went along with cute anyway, and we have stories to tell.

Remember Goodfellas? Robert De Niro told his crew not to buy anything, and they bought stuff. This stirred his anger and he said, "What did I tell you? What did I tell you?" Well, that's what you're going to hear from your family. And one of them will again invoke Robert Ne Niro, "Take it back to where you got it before!"

You don't need a detailed plan from the start. Set a goal and make and outline a plan. When cute comes along they will have to fit into your plan.

Going S.O.L.O

Solo = seek opinions lose objections

When is the truth an insult?

So, we have a course of action that we committed to, but we're not sure about it. We solicit the opinions of others, but only to justify our decision. And, because we already committed, we discard the objections they raise. This is what I call going it solo. If you ask enough people you will get the answer you want.

We tend to "feel" our way into those "next" life events, and then we try to think ourselves out of them. There is a precise path to elevation in out lives. We need to think. We need…

A Plan

This is focused on calculations, not odds. Take into account what you set out to do. Always take stock or inventory the feelings of those you lead or love, as their feelings may have an adverse effect on your life, and you may need to plan accordingly.

There are four factors that will affect your flight plan:

Weight – what are you taking with you? Fear will weigh you down, so you can leave it behind. I know, you are not planning to take it, but it might show up (see lift). Weight can be anything you chose it to be – that's right, you have a choice here.

Lift – the fortitude you possess and employ to overcome the changing variables involved with the success of your endeavor. This would not be your natural disposition. This is what you gain from a period of conditioning for the work. This is Beast Mode.

Thrust – determination. How much force is against your payload? You can view this as the odds to success, examine historical data, inventory your payload (motivation and purpose), and set the expectation.

Drag – simply put, this is resistance. This is not natural like gravity. It's the stuff that people do or do not do that act as distractions. You know how people can drag you down.

But I Have Talent!

What I shared above makes sense, but you have talent, right? You're thinking, my talent will take me to the top. While we can put talent at the top of our rocket, it cannot power the rocket. Too many people make this mistake. You know how we ask, "Whatever happened to so and so with all that talent?"

By contrast, you would rarely ask what happened to the person with determination – you will know about them. They look silly putting together and testing components for a rocket.

Relying on your talent alone will leave the door open for someone else to come along and provide the determination you need. And by allowing this you miss the assembly process, and so it is difficult for you to repeat the initial success. Now, we should look at the kinds of people that will come along to "help" us. Let's call them rocket boosters. They will be determination and thrust for our talent. They offer their services to get you to altitude. By design, they must do this, as they don't often possess our talent.

Rightfully so, rocket boosters fall away at a predetermined point in the flight plan, after expending their fuel. Not so bad, right? – only, operative rocket boosters can cost 60% of a space rocket program. Our speculative boosters can cost as much or more. Look at that, you lose the controlling interest of your endeavor, and you end up working for the person(s) you hired to work for you.

Small Beginnings

I recall seeing a young woman standing outside the subway singing. At first people stopped to watch and listen to her. She was not a great singer and over time people ignored her, but she persisted. Who could do that? I don't think she had singing talent, but she sure had determination talent. Okay, you need talent to take you far, but talent alone will not take you far. We should concern ourselves with things that support our talent. I may not be able to boost my talent myself, but I need to know how it works. People may be attracted to our talent, but many will also be attracted to our income. While I groom my talent, I need to research the industry, read biographies, read contracts, and anything else that can help my talent. It's too easy to get wrapped up in talent, and then launch. Now, we need to rely on others to take care of incidentals. Not a good place to be because their talent will overshadow and control what your talent and attention cannot cover. Some people, if they start feeling like they are being overworked, paid too little, or any other way that an employment relationship can become uneven, they move to correct the perceived shortcoming. I can't take that chance. Let me learn everything involving my career, even if I can't do it myself.

Let's look at a different dynamic. I manage people that could potentially feel this way. The time we spend coaching people under the Applied Leadership model can offset these feelings. When I coach, I am not just building up the person technically and for proficiency, I am building up their self-worth. I am careful to meter out the work so we can review, address, and execute it in sensible parts.

Power Is Not Force

Power is energy and it cannot die. Force, if we apply the definition of life or death, can die because, once the action is taken, the force is over. Force will dissipate after it performs its action.

In the news, there were reports of protests because some police officers were observed using excessive force and having had abused their powers. The protesters were using show of force, which is not uncommon in these situations. Force itself cannot change, but it can change the velocity of an object, and it can change the shape of an object as well. What does this mean in our example? Force can change how quickly events escalate and contort a situation. We can even feel good when we see where our force has moved something away because of impact. It can change the shape of a situation so the worst is not in front of use, but now worse has spread out to the sides of us. People protest because they feel "powerless". And, after the protest, they go home. There is no change because, not long after, another incident happens, and people protest all over again. This has been going on for years. Some will use this sensitive time to their own advantage and riot. In every case you apply force to bring resolution to a problem you get a problem.

Here's another note: if we want to bring calm to an already explosive situation, we should speak in a powerful way not a force way – I think you would agree.

- Power is most used to move people; it can be malevolent of benevolent depending on the wielder.
- Power does not have to be used to be realized.
- Force is an expression of will, usually employed as a means to disrupt.
- Force must be witnessed (perceived as power).

Force is used to remove something from people. Like, dignity, pride, freedom, choice, faith, love, and liberty.

Example: using force in your relationships makes you an abuser. One could argue that using your power in a relationship can be abuse as well, but all things being equal and for the ease of understanding I would like to keep simple. I'll offer this: in your personal relationships, you have the power to influence your significant other.

Power Leadership

We don't lead people by our feelings; we lead people by their feelings. Using your feelings to move people is force but using their feelings to move them is power. It's unproductive and insensitive to get upset and yell at your staff, threaten their jobs, or speak to them in a condescending way. I know, many of us have had the experience of reporting to someone like that. Now, if you do lead people by their feelings, they will see the task through, because it's attached to their feelings.

This will rely on force or a show of strength I'm not engaged in. Leadership should not be based on a show of strength - that is a tactic. This is more like (ego)ship, which we will talk about later. In the Seven Epaulettes of Leadership, I first defined Leadership is a discipline for the leader. Applied Leadership is the method leaders use. Leading people without the benefit of relationship is bullying.

It is possible to lead people through problems. This is based on your love for people – not on your (ego)ship. More on that later.

The use of force is always an unnatural application to a stressful situation or condition. Some may entertain maladaptive coping mechanisms like addictions. And now they must use power (willpower) to beat the addiction. It is my belief that leadership is a discipline for the leader. You, the leader, cannot be led by addiction, and then lead others to your vision. If this should happen, the path to your vision will become polluted.

We may have to move away from doing things to feel good and offset the stress we face. Some people will say, "I need a drink" after a difficult day. Surely, we can see that the drink did not remove the stress, it only distracted us from it. Any time we spend under the influence of an addiction is time not available to our purpose. You see the unnatural application here? We had one problem, now we have another problem. The latter, due to its distracting nature and the fact that we can readily tap into it, may seem appealing, but this is force. We are forcing ourselves into another state of being.

Power Relationships

It's easy to think your spouse doesn't love you if they do not meet your needs. I know of a situation where a husband asked his wife to meet a need he had. The wife tried to meet the need, but she felt the husband wasn't giving her credit for trying. Through more conversation, the husband revealed that he believed he and his wife only worked on the marriage up to the point of getting married.

What was determined is that marriage was the goal, not a happy marriage. Yes, we want to believe the two things are one just as this couple did, but this is not always the case. It would make sense to talk to couples married over 20 years before you marry. We want to identify those things they do and don't do to keep a healthy marriage. Not taking sides, but the wife was secure in the marriage because they achieved that goal. The needs she supplied to her husband were in keeping with her comfort zone. She was working hard and putting forth great effort.

Meet Me Where I'm Going to Be

People like this say: "You never give me credit for anything!" Look, Boo, I cannot give you credit for trying to meet me where I used to be. I need you to be with me, and because I am complicated, I will sometimes need you to meet me where I am going to be. This part doesn't have to be complicated. I know you; I know how you get after your quarterly report. Don't you worry, I have your meal ready, I prepared your clothes, and I'm ready to listen. This is how I show I care. Now, the way I go about caring for you is my love. People seek credit for caring – they seek love for love.

I went a little long on that. Let's return to the good wife. It is important to note that she would return to her last point of reference in the marriage, which was several years ago when she did something for the marriage. The husband is several years hence, and so no matter how much effort the wife puts forth, no matter how well intentioned she was, she could never meet his expectations.

So, you see there? People can work hard for you and expect credit for that while not meeting your expectation. When it comes to love I don't work with credit or fractions. You either love me or leave me alone.

Let me share an example of my Christian walk. You do not need to be a Christian to understand this. Prayer for me was a big production years ago. Comprised of preparation, logistics, structure, research, and intentions. It often started with worship, singing songs to the Lord, followed by a period of praise, and asking for forgiveness (at that time I lived like a monk). After a while, I ran out of things to ask forgiveness for. This wasn't a bad thing as I felt I was showing reverence to God, but I also did these things thinking I needed to do this to be heard. Thinking God would be moved my effort. I might still follow this program from time to time, but I can prayer a sincere prayer. I think much of my time was spent on the effort to please God. I am not so sure I was focused on the relationship. I was more focused on my effort and what I wanted. I am sure there are others that could have adopted the same methodology and got it right.

Now, let's bring it back. I used force to approach God to get prayer answered. I did not harness the power of my faith – force is no substitute for power.

Here is an example of the successful use of power in a "force" potential situation.

Think about a hostage negotiation. Success is not just engaging the bad guy. Success is in preserving the life of the hostage and the bad guy.

Eighty to ninety percent of hostage negotiations end nonviolently. This is great! This means the words of a trained professional are more powerful than the deadly "force" they could use. The bad guy, out of frustration, decided to use force to meet some objective they had.

Believe me when I tell you if people know you can do the work, they will stand watching you work. They will even engage you in meaningful conversation while they stand there and watch you do the work. A part of leading people is growing them to replace you.

Purpose doesn't have a schedule. It creates the schedule.

Makes sense and it sounds cliché, but how many times have we tried to fit purpose into our schedule?

When we fit purpose into our schedule, we treat it as success. I see how we can be fooled into doing this. Purpose calls you back, purpose wakes you up, it helps you give people the benefit of the doubt, and it helps you to put your own doubts in the proper perspective. There is excitement and anticipation for what's next. Sequela, Latin for: what follows. In medical terms this is generally not a good thing, but when affixed to purpose, it means: to take off.

Yes, and nothing man-made escapes the gravity of the earth by happenstance, not even prayer. We need to make a deliberate attempt to move beyond right here and now. The power of my purpose and the application of my will gets me out of bed in the morning.

Chapter 8 – Preparation

Preparation is the Fuel for Life

How many people have spent more time preparing for a date than preparing for a job interview?

Success is like life. It is not a destination – it is the journey. Purpose is the destination. This where you want to end up, but success is what you achieve on the way to purpose. Putting these two words into perspective makes life more enjoyable. If you chase success only, you run the risk of expending your resources with no means to possess your purpose. There are many people who operate in their purpose, but they make it a job, obsessing over its success – that's not as enjoyable. Here's why I say that: success can be fleeting. It can be taken away from you, but purpose is yours to attain or to lose. When we put these concepts into their proper perspective, our motives and motivation will develop accordingly. When I play video games with my son, I revel in victory. He is quick to tell me winning is not everything – it's about having fun. That is a great sentiment, but why does he get so upset when he loses?

Question: how do you have fun if you're losing? Ah, we can change our motivation to learning the game. This way, poor performance is training. But when we play video games, we don't take much time to analyze what went wrong. We do this on the fly and start the next game. But we do that with life too!

Example: we had a bad personal relationship or a bad hire, and then we say: "I'll never get someone like that again. I'll insert a tougher system of checks to avoid this. I'll make it harder for people to get close to me. Essentially, I'll punish the new person who hasn't even appeared yet for what this person did." Know that while this is a learned behavior, this isn't learning. All we did was build walls and refuse to do exactly what we perceive led to failure. In the video game world, there are hacks and video to show you how to play the game. Well, for life issues we have the same thing. My work is not to find the workaround but to discover the work through. Why reduce and adopt a cold-blooded animal approach? What they do is lie in wait at a popular watering hole for animals and pounce on them. If they score a meal one out of eight times, they count that as a success, but they will never go on to promotion and lead others to do the same.

Remember, leaders learn so they can teach others. Anyone who wants to lead people and doesn't want to teach them is cold-blooded. Over the years, I've taught teams the difference between production and being productive. You can work hard and have nothing to show for it. This cycle of doing and not producing is problem every filing team experiences. Slow down, talk to them, coach the people and the problem separately, let them tell you where the pain point is, don't be quick to pick off every problem at the meeting. Resist the temptation to do this. If a team struggled for months and in one afternoon to threw out several solutions, some of will get lost. The first meeting is about the people. They will no doubt need to vent. This first meeting about performance is about them and their well being. Of course, this is assuming that we never coached this team, we are new to the team, or some other performance dynamic presented itself. Much of this book is dedicated to avoid or mitigate this.

Production is working hard and maybe even feeling tired from doing it. Being productive is having something to show for it. If left unchecked, you could have a rebellion on your hands.

I just can't see calling my team into a meeting and saying, "The problem is you all!" It could be the team. By way of someone not understanding the work, or being unable to keep up with the work, and/or not being right for the work. How about this: multiple people at different parts of the production cycle are not fitting well together, for several reasons. The point is there is something, and it is your job to find out what that something is, with the help of the team, of course. Someone on the team will know what the problems are before we do. I don't think sending an email or a memo will go over well. You must lead from the front, take the reins by rolling up your sleeves, and going down there so your people can see you take a first-hand interest in the matter.

Telling people how it's supposed to work, and then telling them they better make it work is not the solution. Your leadership is needed. Get out there and coach! What motivated them before may not work now. That part is critical because you will mentor, then meet the production. You cannot do the inverse of this. If you mentor them first, you will lose them. You may not know the problem or the extent of the problem. If they do, they may not tell you, thinking you are a know-it-all and leaving you to figure it out. That's relationship too! We've done that to someone in a personal relationship – it's like, "Okay, let's see what happens".

Leadership

People fail not because they plan to fail but because it's easy to fail. We all want things easy. Example: we use our phone to talk, text, email, unlock our cars, start the engines, look at what's happening in our homes, check the stock market, read the news, and check our blood pressure. It's easy.

Escaping the gravity of a difficult situation can be as difficult as escaping earth's gravity.

For no reason at all, this endeavor will be difficult. It's not personal but you're trying to escape the gravity of the situation. Just like a rocket engine thrust, you need motivation. You've got to fill yourself up with a lot of motivation – not after the planning is done; you need a big push in order to take off, but this has to start early. You need to fill your tank with as much motivation as you can muster.

Shawn Abrams

Relationship

Your argument is losing steam, but you argue even harder. Reminds me of Tachyons. Remember how on Star Trek they would mention this. The theory of Tachyons is that they get faster when they lose energy. Another thing we know about Tachyons (from Star Trek lore) is that the Romulans use them to cloak their warbirds. Why do all Romulans seem hostile, and quick-tempered? Not like their cousins the Vulcans, who are logical, always appropriate, and intentional. They too have mastered cloaking, but they cloak their emotions – only, they can do this without Tachyons.

Here's a great interview question: which type of person would you prefer to work with, a Romulan or a Vulcan, and why?

This is interesting, the passion of a Romulan v. the logical nature of the Vulcan. I think the Vulcan would make my eight hours uneventful and maybe even boring. The Romulan would no doubt bring a level of excitement that could help to pass the time quicker, but I would prefer the Vulcan. Passion is good but too unpredictable. I'm the kind of person who needs to see results based on my efforts. Now, in my personal life, I prefer the Romulan. I want passion, and unpredictable has its advantages. Sure, passion could be more volatile but that keeps us working to adjust and overcome – not drama, excitement! Since I went down this "what if" road, I'll keep some Tachyons handy to cloak my emotions if I get into a dispute with my Romulan. A Vulcan relationship would just have reasonable discussions about everything; timed, structured, evaluated, signed, sealed, and delivered – boring.

Imagine, my Vulcan providing me with instructions for a walk through the park: "We shall hold hands with fingers interlaced, and arms forming an angle of forty-five degrees."

Cloaking

Cloaking can be a good thing. We've all had the moment where we wanted to express our feelings, but it wasn't the time or place, right? But some person keeps giving you reason to do so.

At work, the cloak is not just shielding our emotions, but also shielding our job from the initiator. If you work with the public, you know what I mean. If you do a bad job cloaking, they call you out on it. If you do too good a job at it, they turn it up a notch to find your breaking point. Displace yourself from the situation. Pretend the initiator is speaking to someone else, and you are the supervisor – what advice and guidance would you offer someone to deescalate? Taking yourself out of the situation will give you more time to think, it will help you come down, and it will also allow the initiator to notice this. Now, some of us have a way of doing this while being a smarty – that doesn't help.

We reviewed cloaking emotions but trying to cloak oneself in a heated discussion in a personal relationship is not a good idea. We may have had relationships where we felt like shutting down and ignoring the other person. Cloaking the problem doesn't work either. Masking things means we must remember to avoid it. Ultimately, you don't have the power to cloak it by yourself, and your significant other can surface it, probably not at a time of your choosing.

I know we can't resolve our problems like they did on Start Trek or even within the time span they could, but we can use their approach. Identify the problem, adhere to the prime directive, try to communicate, analyze your options, and go forth boldly with your best effort.

To my single readers who are looking for that special someone:

Your future is not in securing any one relationship. Myself, I see my future as something I put together that will outlast me. Now, I don't discount the importance of marriage, but when I'm dead, the marriage is over, honey. Marriage is one of those success events on the way to purpose. Children are the future, a good one – they outlast us. What about setting up a scholarship fund for future leaders? I like that too. I don't want the things we like or desire to compete with purpose, as they will not outlast us. The pursuit of success is a distraction to purpose. Other things and people will come, and we can entertain them but in moderation.

I say this because we sometimes try to juggle purpose, with what we need and desire at the same time. And, because our attention, commitment, and resources vary, so too will our results.

The part of my future I don't live to see is my legacy, as defined by my purpose. I think when we put things like this in perspective, we don't get hung distractions, as these things will pass away.

Human Capital: Investments

Coaching helps our direct reports win their small daily battles; mentoring helps them win the war with self. The mentee will often think they cannot do "it". This is where your Applied Leadership comes in. You gave them insight into people and situations, as well as coaching they can draw on. They gained confidence from this. The time you spent coaching them honed their beast mode, the mentoring you did with them will help to unleash it at the right time. One of the main themes of this book is to not shoot for success; instead we should aspire to obtain purpose. Well, we put purpose before success.

One of the hardest things to do is judge the distance and time it takes to achieve our purpose. We sometimes try to hasten the process, fueled by our ambitions and thereby overlooking success. Make success your goal and you could miss purpose. We need to stop and acknowledge the small successes we get along the way. You got through a difficult job application. Great! What did you learn in the process? How can you apply that to your "next"? Or prolong the process by thinking we have time to get started.

Summertime it's not about success. It's about purpose for me specifically conditioning you for your purpose.

The next level requires conditioning.

The most powerful lesson we learn in failure is the conditioning we get to try again. Success is not the opposite of failure; purpose is. However, purpose may not feel like success. We are hardwired to desire success, and we're bombarded with societal influences to obtain success. Money, power, and the like are synonymous with it. And, of course, this is accompanied by imagery of happiness. The difference is this: success is for you and your purpose is for others. Working towards purpose may seem like work; it may not seem as glamorous as some of the things we do for success. If your purpose is to help people, it may be even harder when the people you try to help do not appear to appreciate your effort. This is fine – but trying to manage purpose and success will compromise your ability to achieve both simultaneously.

There are some wealthy people that feel guilty about their wealth, and so they become philanthropists. They're trying to buy a purpose – I said some wealthy people. They may feel like their pursuits caused them to sidestep purpose.

Before I close this chapter, I want to mention a silent killer for leaders, and that is stress.

It is widely believed that stress can shrink the size of your brain and affect your memory.

How leaders cause stress for themselves:

- Micro-managing others
- Not training, lack of training, or training too late
- Setting unrealistic goals
- Falling out of the 80/20 coaching to mentoring approach (mentoring comes after coaching)
- Being too afraid to address shortcomings
- Failing to set the tone for the team (this is a combination of what the team corporately believes, the purpose of the team, setting expectations, forming relationships, after-action reviews, and providing time for rest and reflection.)
- Trying to change people

This is in addition to any external stress directed at you or your team. And, sadly, the stress you bring on yourself can be passed to your team.

I want to show people on how to be leaders. And I want to show some leaders how to be people, because leadership is not about "leading". It's about people. More specifically, the relationships we have with people.

Professional relationships should not be focused on money, standing, or gain. Of course, this sounds like the morally right position to take, but what happens if this kind of relationship is strained due to one or both parties? Without a relationship that's advantageous to both parties to fall back on, you become adversaries.

Similarly, personal relationships are not about love – they too are about people. Once the love haze wears off or down, you will be left with the day-to-day work of maintaining a relationship. This is where love cannot fix the breakdowns that sometimes develop. Love does not fix problems; however, it can help us stay in "safe lanes" not wanting to damage the love. But if you said, "I love this person and I am willing to live with a shortcoming that my significant other possesses", your fear of losing love is greater than the love you profess to possess. Full stop. Now, I would argue if it is love, it will not wilt due to you sincerely expressing your thoughts or position. In fact, working through difficult times will strengthen love.

For personal relationships, we want to effectively express our love, interpret their love, and successfully bridge these two elements. That bridge is the hard part. Bridges are straightforward, meaning they are straight paths suspended over an expanse. The intriguing thought is that when construction began on the bridge there were supports and apparatus in place. And then the work was completed, and the bridge free for travel in both directions. Sometimes bridges are restricted; travel may cease for a period of time. But as long as the bridge remains it represents a connection between two hard points.

I cannot resist the urge to add that some bridges, which were free, may add a toll and others may raise the toll. You do understand this is for the "maintenance" of the bridge?

Priorities are determined by relationships. Have you tried to squeeze in a task for someone you liked or respected ahead of someone else more deserving? Okay, let's not admit it, but acknowledge it could happen. Let's not think that because we're the boss our every whom will be pushed to the top of the list.

Chapter 7 - Quality Control

Knowing What to Reject

This is one of the hardest chapters to write. What one will reject another will gladly accept.

Can we reject an undesirable characteristic or an unwanted action from someone without rejecting the person? Well, we can all answer that question in the affirmative, because we have all done this. We overlooked something or lived with something someone did that we did not agree with. If this is an "after the fact" situation I could address this, but while I am planning my take off to greater heights, I will not allow it. Which one of you would willingly accept a faulty part and hope things work out?

I see it this way, if there is a one-percent chance a part can fail then there is a hundred-percent chance my endeavor can fail. If we are courting and you show signs of cracking, I am out of there. If the courtship is on the longer side and the person is mature enough and aware enough to "hold it together", then they can overcome it.

If you love me so much that you want to rush into a relationship with me, your decision-making is faulty.

Never mind I write books about leadership and relationships. I must prove this to you, more times than not.

Ask them how they define love. If they cannot define it, how can they recognize it? How do they know they love you? If they think the conversation is too (whatever), this is a red flag. Red flags represent potential for problems.

Before you commit to them look at their people. No, we are not all guilty of association, but I would never discount this.

Hunger Pains

When we are hungry for something, we are draw to it, and we draw that thing and all that comes with it into us. I just got chills from that thought! The problem with hunger is, in time, it will cloud our judgment. There is only the hunger. Love begets love, yes, but the hunger for love will not produce love. If you lack the ability to generate a thing within yourself, you will not find it in another. Sure, they can supply what you communicate is the need, but they become your pusher. Look at you, how do you surrender to someone who can leave you and take that love back? I got chills again.

The person you love will teach you about love. Define love for yourself and by yourself. You might find someone while doing this. I have become quite handy at fixing things around my home. I started by watching videos asking home improvement retailers, and people who try their hand at do-it-yourself projects. I gained more knowledge from these pursuits than paying someone to do the work for me. Capiche?

You're A Boss

We should also look at people who hunger for leadership positions. I get it; we want to be in charge. We think we can do it better, there is a lack of effective leadership, we are expected to lead, we feel we have followed someone else long enough, there's more money, and there's power or some other perks. But the hunger for leadership will never be satisfied. This is not like a passion to help people through your leadership. Regardless of your motivation, leadership comes with lesions and lessons. It's the lesions we remember best because they hurt the most. If we are not careful, we can lead with pain – the pain we brought with us. It is our duty to lead others through the pain points they will undoubtedly encounter.

Don't bring the pain and fight it too. This could mean something different to many people reading this. What each person will have to do is different, and you are expected to work that out. It would be wise to continue to read leadership books and articles. Join leadership groups on social media. There, you will find information and stories that can help you to shake off counter-productive feelings.

Are your relationships still orientated toward your vision?

Question: How often do employees receive an orientation? Once, in the beginning of the employment relationship.

Employers usually say a lot of nice things at that orientation, but then everyone gets busy.

The same thing happens in some marriages. Some people will work on the marriage up to the point when they marry. Now we did that let's do some other things. Anniversaries, holidays, and birthdays are not enough to maintain the marriage.

Re-orientate to what you set out to do. You might see there was a deviation from that intention needing care and attention.

In fact, talking about what was promised will remind you to do these things in advance of the session.

The last thing you need is people telling you that you didn't keep a promise.

The Importance of Small Moments.

My son had a tummy ache. I had warned him about snacking on junk all day. Well, thinking he had gas, I gave him some hot ginger tea. It did the trick. And while he was recovering from his pain, he was open to listening to all I had to tell him. I had his undivided attention. I didn't use the time to scold him. Instead, I comforted him where I could. Of course, I was upset that he didn't listen to me, but his failure to heed my warning wasn't the priority, at the moment – he was. I think all people, no matter the age, would feel the same. Those small moments are long-lasting for some people. What we as leaders see as routine when you connect with a direct report where there is a problem can be added to the coaching column. The company may not have made money, we may not have saved a life, but we were able to connect. The sincere effort/approach to fix the problem is just as important as the fix.

Selection

Doing community work, I've had many people who just walked over and said, "Let me help you guys out." My response is always the same: "No thanks, we got it." I want people to ask how they can help. No, it's not semantics. I want the humility of someone who knows how to follow protocol. Not for me, but for the people I serve. In my experience, assertive people talk in an assertive way to the public. I don't want volunteers to tell the public what they need, because the volunteer means well. If you are in a position to help don't judge, and don't give without asking. I prefer smart people for volunteer work, people who know how to meter out supplies. They know how to listen in order to serve, they see the two hands in front of them receiving, and they see all the other pairs of hands in line behind them. I've had some passionate people too. So passionate and emotional that they came with their own vision of the work. And their vision rarely fit into the vision supporting the design of the endeavor. I'm not opposed to working with volunteers who could use some coaching, but it is not a good feeling to spend more time serving your volunteers in the form of coaching than serving the community.

The volunteers are not just submitting to me, they are submitting to the team spirit, the work, and the people we serve. As the leader of the team, I determine if I will accept someone who doesn't initially appear to align with us. Applied Leadership comes to mind. Can I coach and mentor this person? Can the person get along with the other volunteers? I don't know what makes people want to do community work, but I am glad for them. Working with the public has its challenges – we all know that. I think those who choose to volunteer and do it well have superpowers – an abundance of love, a charitable heart, a keen sense of righting a wrong, etc.

But that's other people, what about us?

What's your origin story? You know, every superhero and villain has a origin story, sometimes called a backstory. Usually, some bizarre accident endowed them with superpowers. What is common to both types is something happened, something changed them. Note: The superpower did not make them good, nor did it make them evil. They were predisposed to be that way and used their powers to support their ideology.

Every superhero has an archenemy, right? Well, we don't need one, but I would like to explore that thing about us, which can counter our success and purpose. Our superpower can address this. For example, I am not comfortable with public speaking, but I have an affinity for words and story telling that moves people – that is my superpower. I needed to know my words would be more impactful if I said them. And so, when it is time to speak to a group, I become that super person who has to rise to the occasion and save the day. When not formally speaking to a group, you might find it hard to believe I could do that. What you are good at will be the very thing you use to move beyond your shortcoming. Okay, this is you, what about your team?

There's a symbiotic connection between leadership and relationships – they need each other, or they should need each other.

A Change is Coming

One day, while working from home, I felt this overwhelming stress. Everything was due right now. Pressure will squeeze out whatever is inside of you. For me on this day, it was tiredness. I thought maybe my team felt the same way. I took a moment to look for a Maya Angelou quote, something inspiring. I found this short one below.

On attitude: *"If you don't like something, change it. If you can't change it, change your attitude."*

-Maya Angelou

On the other side of this quote I felt better. Deep thinking is my deep breathing. You may not see this real-time, but when you do, take your Maya Angelou stress break, and reset if you need to.

Can You Make Change?

You can't change people. Only situations can do this. But you can change a situation, which would cause a change in the person. I thought, this worked for me—so maybe it will work for my team. It gave me the opportunity to show my vulnerabilities. It also gave me the opportunity to show how I can work through stress.

Listen to your own pep talks. I once had a staff member who told me the work was difficult and they were disappointed that our constituents were not more accommodating. My solution was to coach them of course. I said that as people, we feel; as professionals, we limit those feelings to the moment. We must move past our feelings to move people beyond theirs. I explained that we do have the operational space and intestinal fortitude for improvement. If our outcomes are missing something then our relationship and leadership is missing something. It was at that moment I realized I had to be that person I was asking them to be. That pep talk gave me my second wind because I was feeling the way my staff member felt.

Ego(ship)

Leaders who find themselves on the wrong side of history are trapped in an ego bubble. I teach about ego a lot because something triggers it, and something else must come along to counter it. Rarely will someone notice this about themselves and make the necessary corrections. It appears this person is aware because their actions and words seem sure, they can even back up what they believe with compelling arguments, but they are ignorant of the shortcoming. No unlearned person can learn themselves.

The Ego bubble is:

- Conceit – when one's opinion of their ability is greater than fact

- Arrogance – when one's worth is greater than everyone else's

- Entitlement – the expectation of something not deserved

- Greed - pursuit of excess, for self

Take time to outline this because many of us quit jobs or people for one of these reasons. It is common to feel short-changed in a job or a relationship. Examine how you feel after you left. Were you the "only" one working, the only one loving, the only one who knew what was going on? Did you expect to gain something you didn't work for? I am always amazed at people who put the brakes on their work because they were passed up for a promotion. But they slack off at work; nobody's looking so I can get away with something, or they have a "whatever" attitude. They think it's their secret, others don't know so their elevation to the next level should be predicated on the fact that they want it. And so, they go from relationship to relationship, from job to job doing the same things and expecting a different outcome.

What ego is to leadership the critic is to the ego. Naysayers are all around. They talk to you as you tote your rocket to the launch pad. Critics watch from a safe distance. If they talk about you after you take off – it's fine. If you let the naysayers get to you, you will restart your countdown over and over because of their fears. They don't have what it takes for the success of your mission, and they don't have your purpose. Maybe what we're doing is not impressive to a lot of people. Look, someone won the Nobel Prize in chemistry this year, and I know they're not waiting for me to congratulate them. Building for success is for your fans and ego.

I did this very thing, for a short time. Trying to get people to notice me. Playing humble but secretly wanting accolades. That might look like success, but that's not purpose. The more you do this, the more you want it. And, the more it seems your success is in people seeing it and saying it. Trying to maintain this mindset or maybe I should say heart-set fuels the ego(ship) not the rocket ship. The problem with the ego(ship) is you don't need to go anywhere – you have already arrived. Well, this was uncomfortable for me and I wasn't good at it – I failed miserably. It wasn't enough for me to experience setback. But my problems were like, "Abrams, it's time to give you some disrespect." Ego.

The Bubble

We all have active imaginations, dreams; and we hold a vision of what we want in the future.

Remember our theme: **Feel, Think, and Act.**

Imagination and dreams can make us think and feel, but we seldom act on them. Vision, while like the other two, is in a class by itself. Because it will end with us taking action. Here's an example: Someone could imagine that they failed or, perhaps they imagined their plan failed, but this doesn't make them go out and do anything. By contrast, no one has a vision of failure. Vision is bigger than failure. Vision is a deliberate decision we make to see the future as we would like it to be, which can include purpose, if we know what that is. Our imagination and our dreams tend to creep up on us – they are thoughts we must contend with.

Make note of what comes next. The dot.com companies of the 90's that came and went quickly. It's called the dot.com bubble. They mistakenly thought they had a vision of the future. Since what they saw was big, they embraced a dream opportunity. Notice I said they saw "dream opportunity" and not a vision. Okay, opportunity was the bubble, and their interest and money expanded it. And when the ambitions of these companies and their investors exceeded the dream opportunity, the bubble burst. What's interesting about is that you might not see this coming, if you do, you don't know when the bubble will burst; however, you will only know that this happened. Yes, these are rearview mirror events. And this is how we know it wasn't vision. There, I answered the question you didn't ask. I think ego is a large factor in the boom before the burst. In business, optimism is not being prudent. It's, "do this again and do it more."

Relationship bubbles are the same. We place a high valuation on the person and the relationship, and because of this, we invest much of what we have thinking this is safe. The more I put into this the better it will be. Our relationship investments should be metered out (everything in moderation) based on expectations, response, information, trust, evidence, potential, and capacity. This is not vision; this is blind sight reasoning. If we go down this road, ego becomes involved. And we stay the course to save the relationship or save face. We may even take drastic measures to exit, again, to save face but also our resources.

It's your vision but you have to speak the language of the people.

You'll need to explain your vision to them, using a narrative packed with illustrations. Recall how great orators (motivational speakers) make you feel, think, and act with their words. They tell a story which takes you our of your resting state. You feel empowered to do something. Now, if you have instructions and a goal included, you have not only a team – you have a movement. Your meetings and instructions should be told in story format. You have an opening scene, characters, plot, conflict, climax, antagonist, protagonist, and denouement. At some point during your discourse, you will ask good questions. President John F. Kennedy illustrated this brilliantly when he said, "Ask not what your country can do for you, ask what you can do for your country." I love that! You don't want to answer the question directly for them. You already shared what you want done. You want to leave them with the story and the question to mull over. The compelling story will keep them anchored in your vision and the question will keep them looking for ways to answer by working towards it.

I think this method effectively transports the listener to your vision. They not only see it, they see themselves there as a part of it.

Oh, Lonely Days

Our ego is lonely because it doesn't like keeping company. It likes witnesses. "I need people to see me, I need people to acknowledge all I do," and all the rest. And, because ego is not a physical place, it can never be filled.

Force, like ego, needs an audience to bear witness – that is its true power.

Now, ego can drive people to complain, and it can resort to the use of force to express itself. Complaining to raise awareness is fine, but complaining without securing the means to effect change, either by default or design, will move people to avoid your cause. You will be viewed as a complainer for your cause. When you secure the means for change, and apply it, you become a campaigner for your cause.

Have you ever had a public setback, and then you thought, "I need to prove to all who saw me fail that I can do this?" Caution: They were not designed to be the fuel that drives you. By using them for this purpose you run the risk of overshooting your objective. Ever try that same thing again and fail in front of the same people? See what I mean? The person more concerned with impressing people than purpose or even success will fail and fall face-down-pants-pockets-up – now the apex of the effort is the floor of the effort.

Suggested reading: *Robert's Rules of Order*

The Weight is Over

Don't make an escape capsule heavier than the rest of your rocket. You could end up with a nice, shiny finished product, but struggle to take off. The fact that we are trying something new means we need to make space for new. I know, we're a little afraid (a lot), we think things will still work out (hopefully), and generally see we feel we can start right now (maybe). We're not making space for failure, which is what doubt and fear do. A porous plan will collapse on itself. It doesn't matter who or what came up against us.

Ted Kennedy was once asked by a reporter, "Why do you want to be president of the United States?" The long pause before his answer rang louder than the words that would follow. It cost him. In our lives, we must be careful of people who speak complex(ese) to us to get some benefit, but struggle to answer the simple questions. Try it – why do you want to be with me? Why do you want this job? Why should we build it? Who knows, maybe they don't want what they are selling, and they are even trying to talk themselves into it. I prefer to struggle with the questions and answer instead of struggling with this person and their proposal. Senator Kennedy was a great American and had a great career in the senate, but at the time he ran for president he may have been running not for his ego, but his family's.

Ego driven love is "all about me": I withhold love for you and maybe even ignore you so you will show me attention, but I was wrong in the first place because I don't love myself. I can't get you to love me and this is all about attention. It's not about love. I don't love myself. I just want to feel good about myself so you can. You can see love, but you want the emotion of love that's all encompassing, but that's not present in me. I need to get that from people, so I engineer a situation where I can solicit the feelings of love, which is really the attention I crave so that I can feel good to feed my ego, which completely misses the emotion of love.

Earlier, we learned that stress could shrink our brain. Fear can weigh us down.

Controlling Interests

Considering options is the process of decision-making, but considering decisions is controlling the outcome. Right there, you have lost. You are not the outcome; the outcome is external to you.

God gave man dominion of the earth and all things in the earth, but not mankind. To control a person or a people is inherently against the order that God set. Control is not leadership or love – it is fear. The most powerful force in all creation gave us free will. And the opposite of that is control.

Consider nations that control their subjects. The leader determines what makes the people happy.

What is Happiness?

Internal dialogue: I never defined this. I only said this within myself or to others when I felt it. Some people make the conscious decision to be happy. Sometimes after a bad relationship or some other disappointment.

You know, if you ask most people whether or not they're a leader, they're going to tell you yes they are. But, if you ask those same people to define leadership, they're going to struggle. Question: How is it possible to maintain the integrity of a thing if you can't define it? How can you teach it to others or even receive it yourself? Leadership is a discipline for you, the leader, not the people you lead. Applied Leadership this is the methodology we use to effectively lead people. It's comprised of two parts or two practice areas that are mentoring and coaching. Coaching is where you go to the person. You know, you meet the person where they are figuratively. This is key because you're coaching the person's emotions, but mentoring is where you bring the person to where you are – maybe you assign them something that you would never do yourself or something that represents a next step for them. So, we coach emotions of the person, but we mentor them mentality. We have to be mindful that to move someone from their thinking to our thinking would also move them out of their comfort zone, which I call their nest, and that is mentoring. Most of the time we spend with the people we're leading should be spent coaching, as this is where the relationship lives. It's the day-to-day conversations and concerns they have. And mentoring is a test of how well we presented the coaching, and how well they received the coaching. Remember this: 80/20 split coaching versus mentoring. But this is where the problem occurs in our professional and personal lives or relationships, we do the inverse – we do 20% coaching and 80% mentoring. Most of our time spent mentoring is challenging because mentoring people is challenging. You're challenging the person, and there's nothing wrong with challenging someone, but we have to prepare them for the challenge before we present it to them. It doesn't matter what age they are, or how educated, or even their relation to you. Let's say you ask your significant other, "Why did you do that or why didn't you do what I asked you to do?" and they respond, "Look I'm frustrated." And you say you're frustrated. "I'm frustrated. Why can't you do what I asked you to do?" Does that sound like coaching? No, and it's not really mentoring, but it is closer to mentoring because it's challenging the person. We want them to lead the way they're thinking and think the way that we're thinking. It's not a true example of mentoring, but it's closer now we know that person is not ready to change their thinking yet. That's why we have to go back to the coaching part that's the 80/20 split in favor of coaching. And it's not 80% of your time, it's 80% of the time you spend with the person is spent coaching them. You don't have to tell him what they should be doing – that's not coaching. One way of coaching is to ask open-ended questions and just listen. You can just be there for them. You want them talking to you and feeling they can talk more, express or share their feelings, and their thoughts with you. If they cannot do this, they will hold it in. The worst thing that could happen if someone holds in their thoughts is, eventually, they must lie about them, not wanting to cause alarm or disappointment. The worst thing that could happen after holding onto their feelings too long is these feelings might quickly surface without decompressing, and – Bam! Blow up! Right there at the party, at the family reunion, at the worst possible time, and now after a lot of talking and a lot of shedding tears everyone wants to start coaching each other. They will begin asking each other, "How do you feel, how are you feeling?" And when they get the response they say, "Oh, I didn't know that. I didn't know you felt that way, you should have told me!" You might be thinking, "Well what's the big deal if you can coach on the back end? You can still patch things up." No, it's better to have a coaching program, a sustained practice of coaching in your relationship to avoid problems in the first place. If you say better late than never, I will say better early than ever. You might have to rewind that; it sounded weird, but it makes sense.

Okay, we talked about leadership, we talked about Applied Leadership, but where are we leading people? Now, we'll talk about Vision, which is the future as we would like it to be. Please note if we are not leading people to our vision, we are leading them to our ego. You don't like what I said. Example: Parents may have said to their children, "Do as I say because I'm your parent and you have to listen to me!" See, there is no mention of vision – only, you must do as I say, which means I lead, you follow me, but who is the "me"? That is your ego. Again, there is no vision, this is just you and your ego, but your child, receiving this information, might be thinking, "Yeah, but I don't want to be like you." I know, that's hard to hear too, but if we're not coaching, we won't know what they're thinking. Coaching is not mentoring. And leadership without the benefit of relationship through coaching is bullying. This is a situation where you can have relationship through coaching, but you opt out of it in favor of just telling someone what to do because of your authority. So, parents, coaching doesn't have to be work, for you don't need a computer or white board. You can just talk to your kid, but mostly listen. And you don't have to make suggestions and comments every time they say something; you do not have to interrogate them, dig deeper, and get granular in every conversation. Just let them say what they have to say and when they finish say thanks, give them a hug, and then go do their laundry – I'm kidding.

YouTube| The Seven Epaulettes of Leadership | Video: 17b (check)

Chapter 6 – Look Both Ways

Are you a window gazer or a guage gazer?

If you want to be a star you look at the stars–not clouds.

mean, the temptation to look out of the "window" is great. You want people to see you. If you work hard, you're looking to escape your circle your neighborhood or town. You want to look out the window if you want to see what's there, but why look at anything short of the goal that keeps you bound?

You need to be looking at where you want to go, not all the places you want to pass. Have you ever driven in an unfamiliar place, focused on the directions, the next turn, and your destination, and missed your turn? Okay, stay with me. Then you turned around and exit headed in the opposite direction to try again, but you missed that exit too? Yeah, that happened. Imagine if you were in a rocket and did that. Your chemtrail would look like the Fantastic Four symbol. No, I'm not trying to sneak conspiracy stuff in here; it's just an illustration. If you want to be a star, you look at the stars – not clouds, and certainly not the people on the ground looking at you.

T-Minus Everything and Counting

Experienced pilots fly by instruments because you cannot trust your eyes, and, coming fast, you see the vision clearly, but the path to the vision is blurry. This should be so because you are moving fast. If your gauges are calibrated and you planned and plotted properly, you can focus on your ascent.

We need to gauge, effectively, how much time should be spent on metrics (the gauges).

You know, like when you're talking to your neighbor. You can only do that for about ten minutes before you're ready to go inside. The same thing is true at networking events – after ten minutes you need to move on to others. You're getting information right now to make decisions, right now or in the future. To stay there, fixated on the information, will increase doubt and fear. No, don't make hasty decisions.

Gauges are good, but too many are a distraction. You only need to glance at your speedometer. Some gauges will tell you how much you have left or have used (depending on how you see that sort of thing), and some gauges are redundant like the tachometer in an automatic car. You don't need to know the revolutions of your transmission, because you're not shifting, but without it you'd have a huge hole in your dash.

Social media sites they have dashboards with tons of metrics. Initially, the information is helpful, but after a while you decide which gauges to look at the most. Too much information is difficult to process. It will lead to second-guessing, delayed decisions, regret after a decision is made, and ultimately may prove to be a distraction.

Too many people have a moral compass that is set to Ego. Understandable, as so many things can drive us to pursue success – like fear, previous failure, jealousy, deception, hurt, etc. This moral compass is stuck on ego. There is no degree of ego, no fuzzy logic. I don't see this as a gauge. It's more like a trick mirror. You see yourself and because that is what you want to see, you think you are fine. Well, to each his own.

Spending most of the relationship time in your own head?

If you find yourself explaining what love is to your significant other, you have a problem – a capital condition. If they did not represent love in the beginning, what did you fall in love with? Ah, so we can't blame them. Perhaps the pretense of the relationship took place in our minds, and then after we met this person in the physical, we continued to project onto them in our mind. Now, we flashback into the physical to ask, "Who are you?" Truth is, they may not have changed at all.

So, if you are showing love and you find yourself explaining love, you are doing both parts of the work. Imagine, math class, you have been assigned a partner, you are doing all the work, and yet you both share the grade. People talk about "luck up" in marriage. I would prefer to love up. Love will outlast any amount of luck. For those already in a committed relationship, I don't say leave it, but do leave "it" to prayer. For those of us on the near side of such a situation, we have time to re-orientate our thinking before major disappointment.

I'm sure one day someone will develop an app that will monitor our biorhythm for truths about us. That could be good, but in case someone is working on that right now, pay attention to my example. I put on my smart device, leave home, travel to work, and walk into a meeting. When I sit down someone asks, "Abrams, why are you late?" And my device reports, "Abrams woke up late after not getting enough sleep last night, left the house late, spoke with his neighbor for ten minutes, returned home five minutes after leaving for an unknown reason, spoke to a neighbor for two minutes, and stopped to consume a food item, which exceeded the daily sugar allowance." Silence fills the room as everyone is listening, and then my device says, "Elevated stress levels detected."

Success, or that vertical we want to make will be uncomfortable. Astronauts trying to leave earth's gravity must travel three times the gravity or earth or three g's to escape the earth.

What is gravity? It's a powerful pulling force that comes from mass. The more mass, the denser that mass is, the greater the gravity. People can be the gravity pulling us. Yes, the people we surround ourselves with make it hard to escape them. Look at that, it's hard to be with them and it's hard to leave them. With people it's not this invisible force, it's the mindset they have; their conversation has to keep you with them. They won't engage you in topics that will launch you to novel altitudes. Why would they? They haven't been there themselves.

Why are you operating at their altitude for? To escape the gravity of the earth requires different thinking.

In aggregate, we are not limited to what we know or what we see today. That's an important thing to understand since it's hard for us to fathom – because life beyond the limitations of what we understand operates at a different set of rules.

I know, you want to go higher faster, but ascending too quickly in the literal sense of the word can give you altitude sickness. With respect to your relationships, leadership, and goals, the best way to encounter as little unpleasantness as possible is to take it slow. To escape the gravity of the earth requires different thinking – altitude thinking.

Change of Concept

High altitude thinking allows you to look down or back on our current situation from a different perspective. This is important because perspective comes from experience and disposition.

When experience and reference are grounded, we look up to see the bottom of the success. Purpose is beyond that, and in order to think differently we must perceive differently.

Beyond the veil of failure – that's gravity. You will know when you reach that point (escape velocity) when you experience pain points.

It is possible to lead people through problems. Don't stop to feel the pain points. You can experience it, fine, but to stop and complain about it or to assign blame is pointless. This would be as effective as using a rain chain to fix a leaky ceiling.

It takes a lot of effort to compartmentalize the disappointment of what did not work for you and still throw your full effort behind someone else to do the same. I don't know about you, but I like looking at the same work through a new set of eyes.

You didn't choose your problem and you don't have the solution to the problem, but you can choose how you live with your problem.

Choose

You're in the race, but are you running in the right direction?

I had a graphic made for my blog that could tell the story in a visceral way. The graphic depicts several runners at the starting line in a race. All but one runner is facing the right direction. You see, they are all there, in the right place, at the right time, all prepared and ready to go, but one person is facing the wrong direction. This illustrates the point that we can show up for a relationship but run right back into the past. Has this happened to you? You realize you're going wrong, but because you're upset you go even faster and harder just out of frustration.

No, not you? Okay, what about this one: You're in a heated discussion and suddenly realize you're wrong. You can't stay on the wrong path, but you've already invested too much emotion. Rather than do a full reversal, you change the direction and come up with some unflattering revelation about them. Okay, we looked at how we go against the norm and ourselves. Let's now take a look at how we perceive people who are against us.

Everyone who doesn't jive with you doesn't have to be against you. You two just might not see eye-to-eye. It's your job as their leader to ascertain this and take steps to correct it. There's some shortcoming with or within the person, but it's not directly related to you, it just surfaces when they connect to you. I don't propose that leadership is the direct fix for this – that's what relationship is for.

The coaching is where the hard work is, that's where the relationship lives. That's the hard part – it's ensuring that you're available to make as many connection points from them to yourself as possible. That way, if the one connection you have fails, you will still be connected. With just one connection, you must be quite flexible, patient, tolerant, respectful, understanding, and forgiving.

I'm sure we've all had the experience of someone connecting to a raw nerve of ours. For them, this may not mean anything, but for you, it may cause times when you want to sever the connection. Not if you lead them. You're not just leading them to achieve your vision. You are charged with helping them to develop and achieve their own. The mark of a great leader is someone who can push past disappointment, examine how they feel, then take decisive steps to move past them and continue leading. How potent your leadership is will be determined by your ability to move your people forward, and how well you lead them through "forward".

Pass the Buck Or Make the Change

Okay, we just looked at perception, and we looked at how training via corrective action is not always the solution unless the problem is based on performance. If an entire team is underperforming, you must look at the goals, the logistics involved with achieving goals, and your own leadership. You don't get to be leader and blame the people. Imagine, being the president and blaming the people in your cabinet, everyone that reports to the people in your cabinet, and the people in your nation – that would be absurd.

Without good leadership there will be judgment and blame, plain and simple. The leader will blame people, people will blame people, and some will blame the leader. Whether good leadership or bad, the leader will take the blame for any shortcoming. If your entire team is failing or just one, it's your problem.

The solution to an underperforming team is leadership. Leaders must teach leadership, your leadership. If for no other reason than this: They must lead their team out of the low place. It's a low place for their mental state, as well as their productivity. What is the status of your relationship with them? Is there is any animosity? You cannot put a good plan on bad feelings. Watch this: I'm sure a number of leaders can read this book, apply much of what they learned, but have different results. It's not the leadership training at fault. How you employ and deploy what you possess as a leader is innately you. It's not just what you learn, it's how you use it. You will always make the difference for your team's success.

If your team is struggling, inventory your feelings and ask them to do the same. Share talk about it. This is the relationship part. Look for comparisons and make note of how these are significant. You know what's coming next, right? Look at the differences and explore why we feel differently about the same failed event. It doesn't have to be that anyone is wrong for what they are feeling, but giving them the opportunity to share and, more importantly, to discuss this will help everyone to shake "it" off. No plan on this day, just make sure they know you care about how they feel, and that it is more important to you than what didn't work out.

I built my first rocket two years ago when I wrote the book, "Leading in the First Person". It was okay for a first attempt. I made videos to accompany it and enjoyed a measure of success. The second rocket was "The Seven Epaulettes of Leadership". This rocket saw refinements, and, as you can imagine, it was more successful. But after I began to market the book, I realized this wasn't my purpose. This is how I have come to say that success is on the way to purpose. Success grew steadily with maturity and experience. This third rocket is the most powerful I have built to date. It too is not purpose, but another step towards it. Every nation that has a rocket program has gone through this same process of development. And, they announce this. Every nation that built a rocket to go to outer space has used it to put satellites into orbit. This is useful, satellites allow us to see far away, and they allow us to see each other with more closely. Now that what we see worries us, we put nuclear weapons on those rockets and announce this to the world as well. Mankind can turn every advancement into a tool for destruction. What will you do once you reach that next level? How will you use the new insights you gained?

That time I saw brilliance in my mother.

I learned grace and dignity from my mom. I saw her praise God all night when her youngest son passed. I marveled at the sight of this woman, praising the God she had prayed to, just hours before, to heal him. That prayer wasn't answered, but He is still her God. I get my passion to help people from my mom too. Ah, but my drive to help people, that comes from the pain of my problems. "Mama told me there would be days like this", but she didn't say there would be quite so many. Old school people had a short way of talking to you. They didn't have to take all afternoon to make a point. What they had to say was short and sweet. Followed by, "Do you want to be like so and so?"

I thought I knew my mother, but on that night, I saw loyalty, devotion, leadership, relationship, faith, and peace. You don't forget those moments; they shape you in unknown ways. Well, I don't want to define how it shaped me. I just know I am different because of it.

Interlude

I'm from Brooklyn, New York. I grew up at a time when slap boxing was poplar among urban youth. Unlike ring boxing, where your footwork is the paramount, slap boxing uses your upper body more. It's a lot of head faking and shoulder rolls. And, of course, your hands are open to better slap your opponent. Also, for some reason, you had to make hissing sounds to coincide with your strikes. You had to slap-box three people just to leave the block you lived on. What the bigger kids didn't know is that they were preparing younger guys like myself for hard life lessons. I'm not glorifying the activity, but you learned it was advantageous to have quick hands, or as a last resort, quick feet. The latter was a poor choice as running away would only make the mob angry – I learned to stand and fight. This deliberate act would gain you some respect, which was just as good as a win. One day, my mother sent me to the store to buy her some pantyhose. On the way, I was only stopped once and ordered to "throw my hands up" – I earned my pass. I got the pantyhose, and, on the way back, the bag was so light it blew in the wind. The neighborhood boys, curious about the contents of my sailing bag inquired about it.

T-Minus Everything and Counting

They didn't believe that "nothing" was in the bag, and in no time at all the whole block knew what I was carrying. They all lined up to slap-box me, even the girls got in line. That was a bad day, but most days were okay. In time, I learned that I had stamina. Over the years, this made up for my lack of technique and speed. I had become too much work for a fight, let alone a win. And so, I would get a pass because I was not easy. I lost a lot of these playful matches, but no one would call me a loser – I told you, I am not a loser. I am a fighter. Now that I'm an adult, with bigger problems, I see know more than ever the importance of the fight for personal growth. I might not have all the answers for my problems, but I believe I possess the stamina to outlast them.

abramsindex 404 | March 20, 2020

This time in my life was the first launching pad I can recall. From here, I would go on to make a big decision for my future. The launch pad is a secure footing. It is the final stage before you take off. Something profound brought you to this point, and something profound will happen when you leave the safety of it. On the launch, there is no judgment, no help – there is only the expectation.

Slap boxing. Have you even been in a situation where you fully analyzed and appreciated how difficult it was before your fight or flight reflex could kick in? Well, that was my moment. My brain synapses were firing – it seemed as if the entire afternoon passed me by as I stood there thinking what to do next. Only seconds passed by, but I recognized all the ways someone could fight. You can fight to win, fight to a draw, fight for your life, or fight just to fight. Well, the unpleasantness of the situation did not last long, but I thought about those options for a long time. Not all our thoughts shape us immediately – in my case I had to grow and mature into what this would eventually mean to me. Having many options to choose from removed the fear I had held.

Chapter 5 - By Design or Default

When a conversation on my team surrounds disappointment in a setback, then disappointment in all the effort we put to achieve something but failed, that's a case for leadership. It could be training as well, but my team needs coaching, they need mentoring. I need to get their minds right before we can look for a new plan because the worst thing to do is release a great plan when people are feeling bad. It may not have the same effect of motivating them. Motivate first, and then release the plan.

Leadership

Relationship

We all hold on to bad moments, bad memories, and bad feelings, but some of us amass a warehouse worth of them. They are like hoarders. Hoarding begins long before we see the physical evidence. It appears to be a warehouse full of this stuff until there's no space for good memories, is no clear and free space to pack up a lot of good memories.

Imagine working in this warehouse, walking by all of these bad memories and all these bad feelings. Even if a good memory came in, you wouldn't have space to put it anywhere. It doesn't go with bad feelings from a personal relationship, that feeling from the boss, bad feeling from the commute to work. There has to be a new space to put it in, but it doesn't seem like you should go to the effort of putting this one good memory someplace when you have all these bad memories all around you. So what do you do? Eleven in a mile and on occasion when you're traveling through the warehouse of bad memories you pass by it and you might say, "Oh yeah, that good thing happened." But then you continue on to get to a big mountain of bad feelings. That's hoarding.

Hoarding is not just a physical thing and doesn't just take place in the physical. Hoarding actually takes place in your mind before you buy 10,000 antique teacups. You already had the condition to do this and to sustain it, and there's something about releasing it you cannot do. Stop. Someone gave you something valuable, like, I don't know, an expensive painting. You would look at the painting and go, "Well, I don't know if I have a space for this. It's not really my thing." So you might reject it because your life is full of teacups and that's your thing.

But for the person who just pours emotion, we don't get to see it because it's not visible around us. They carry it in their mind, and, at some point when you engage them, they walk through all their bad memories and bad moments and bad feelings, acknowledging them as they traverse their warehouse on the way to you. They remember all these bad things and they get to you and say, "What?" And you say,

"Good morning." And they say, "What's so good about it?" And you say, "Thank you very much."

Emotional Investment

Facebook allows you to donate to someone's favorite charity on their birthday. I thought, "What a novel idea." However, my circle of friends doesn't get the large amount of money assigned to their goal. That's because the effort doesn't look successful if a small amount is obtained and a large amount is expected. Starting at zero is not appealing to anyone, even if it's support for you. Given that the money would be used for a good cause doesn't sway us. You need to be more than fifty percent to get support. People are more inclined to support not because you start something, but because it looks like you will be successful in your pursuit. We're not fickle for this reason - it's hardwiring. While humans are the dominant species on this planet, there are a lot of things that can kill us. And, we associate risk with our mortality, fiscal responsibility, quality of life, legacy, pride, etc. In the case of a bank loan, we need collateral. How much? Try assets that total one hundred percent of the borrowed amount. Even then this doesn't mean the bank thinks you will be successful. Their concern is to recoup what they gave you.

In a personal relationship, we look for emotional collateral. Does this person have the ability to return my emotional investment? Of course, they would say, "yes" and could cite all the things they did for their last person, but that's not attractive to hear. And so, we calculate their potential emotional investment based on what they say on a rolling basis. Let's examine this closely. If what they offer in terms of Emotional Investment is far in the future, watch out. This means you must wait to see it, and it could be a long time. Too much time to recall all the details and too much time for them to propose intimacy, which will change the equation. If they don't have a job, but they tell you what they will do for you once they do get a job, you're taking a risk. If you close that deal, they will never get a job, live off you, and leave you to wait for the promise. If you really care about me, put yourself in the best position to give me the best. Anyway, we all want love, and anyone who's cute with a convincing conversation seems like more than fifty percent – tell the truth. For some, their story reads like this passage. And you know what? They won't like what it says. Now they don't like this book, and now they don't like Abrams for writing it. Notice I did not say leave them today, I did say "think". Are you still waiting for a promise made years ago? It's worth a sincere conversation.

What's the Anti-matter with You?

Norwegian author, Aksel Sandemose, wrote the book, "A Fugitive Crosses His Tracks in 1933". He writes about a fictional society that holds the collective as more important than an individual. This is defensive thinking at its best. It's safer for those who do not want to apply themselves if no one tries to improve themselves. This cloak of nothing is a defensive measure, a tomb for the society inside it, and worse for the individuals of that society.

We may subconsciously resemble one or more of these laws. Seeing them listed here could be jarring.

Believe it or not, some countries subscribe to this thinking and attribute it to a high score on the happiness index. I don't know if this is art imitating life or life imitating art.

I was born in a different time and place. My belief system is different, and, after all, I teach leadership, relationships, and purpose. I would be open to debate with a champion of Jante Law while being careful not to attack what they believe. Hey, they attribute their happiness to it.

The ten fictional, but relevant, laws of Jante may not be known to many people outside of Norway. Here they are:

The Law of Jante:

- Do not think you are anything special.
- Do not think you are as good as we are.
- Do not think you are smarter than we are.
- Do not imagine yourself better than we are.
- Do not think you know more than we do.
- Do not think you are more important than we are.
- Do not think you are good at anything.
- Do not laugh at us.
- Do not think anyone cares about you.
- Do not think you can teach us anything.

These laws fall under the Defensive Thinking Mindset. I say under because if you are being defensive, you are protecting yourself. These laws seem to betray the natural inclination of self-preservation of the subscriber. In fact, that is the case. The collective is greater than the individual.

Face the Fire

The most exciting part of a rocket launch is the firing of the engines – the explosion of fuel, and power.

You cannot reason with angry, uncontrollable people. If you could, they would not be angry or uncontrollable. Instead, you must talk to them in feelings. We think and remember in pictures. The pictures you must to take them need to emotionally offer a safer place to deescalate. Where they are in the moment that they're upset is not a safe place. Trying to rationalize it or make it logical is not going to make it better. If I told you that I were in a fire because I feel like I'm in a fire and you try to explain the fire to me I would think you are crazy. I will try even harder to tell you that I'm in a fire. I would yell and I would act out in an animated way.

The analogy is a correct one because the person feels they're in a fire. You clearly see this is not the case, but you want to let them know it's okay for them to feel that way – and you have to understand that if they feel like they're in a fire, they don't feel like they can guide themselves out of it. They're busy thinking about the fire, not escaping from the fire.

Vengeance and "I want to burn you in that fire" are not enough to let you learn they want to see you burn.

You wouldn't try to fan the flames of the fire. You wouldn't even try to make the person come out of the fire because you don't want to. You need to help the person find an exit from what they feel. It's hard, but the solution is not withdrawing from the conversation because that's like abandoning someone in a fire.

That's a poetic example. I know it was long, but I made it sound nice, right? But that didn't help the fire situation, so talking long and saying nice words doesn't help the situation either.

Now, we don't know the cause of the fire the person is experiencing. It could be us or the fire could have been burning for this person long before and the source is someone or something else. Well, that may be the case, but your words could be the flash point.

The flashpoint is not a hot temperature. It could be the lowest temperature. What's the vapor? Something that's hard to see, something that's nearly intangible, something that can go undetected, quickly flashing over. Don't let your words be a current that causes the flashpoint.

This post did not perform well on Twitter, but I don't care. It's my book.

Fires dancing wildly with reckless abandonment. It is ignitable sources that set the stage.

Make safe passage so that both of you may egress safely. Even if you do not feel like you want to, the fact that you both escaped the fire is more important.

Someone, if you abandon them burning in a fire and they survive, they will get you.

The problem with withdrawing from someone when they're in their fire is that your physical body will survive it – and don't forget they're going to bring it back. That fire will continue to burn. If they have an opportunity, they're going to try to engage with you.

You should know this about a fire: the faster a fire burns the hotter it is. And so, it would be fair to say that people with quick tempers generally get over-the-top angry. Can people be ice cold, and still on fire? Absolutely! Example: "Are you okay?" Response: "Yes. I. Am. Fine. There is nothing wrong. Everything is great!"

Fire transforming sweet memories into sour reality

The apology must ring louder than the disrespect.

Rest and reflection are the new "r and r". We do monthly and quarterly reports for work, why not do this for us? What were the things (metrics) you want to analyze and make note of in your life or relationship? Example: I reduced my salt intake by twenty-five percent. I made intentional efforts to move my negative thoughts fifteen times. I read two books. I saved two hundred dollars on my insurance bill – a joke; I couldn't help it. This is your self-love/self-care, which is the best thing you can do to fight the ego trap. You see, if you're busy taking care of you, there would be no desire to abuse people to feel good about yourself or better than others.

I learned that you cannot lead people to the present; you must lead them to the future. Not someday, today.

Confabulations!

This is where your mind will recall information that did not happen to make sense of an event. Studies show that, as we get older, we become more prone to this as well.

I think this happens to couples too.

Have you ever had a disagreement with your spouse and later you both recall totally different facts about the disagreement and the thing that caused the disagreement?

When times are good, there is a high probability you two will share the same recollection. But if there is a row between you two, not only will you two recall differently, you will take turns correcting each other.

Anticlimactic

Know this, people evaluate relationships based on how it benefits them. You might have a different view. You might think, "This benefits both of us."

Example: You might think an employee should be happy or content because they have a job. But that's not enough to maintain a relationship. This is a situationship, and it can end without warning, or the standard two-week notice. I know, people move on for a number of reasons, but if the surprise of it leaves you thinking, "I didn't see that coming!" You may not have had a relationship, or it may not have been the kind you thought it was. I had a great working relationship and decided to leave my employer, but I was afraid to tell my boss – she was a great supervisor and friend. But, get this; she couldn't bring the value I needed to our working relationship. I knew this was a situationship because I had outgrown my position and there was no other for me to assume. While I was there, I did all the relationship things had to, out of respect for her, the company, and myself.

What I experienced is not uncommon. Once "value" is determined, and it is met or exceeded, that's it. Even gold, as important as it is, cannot be revalued. Some companies think they set a "gold standard" for employee well being, again, since they offer employment. Gold (the precious metal gold) does have a standard. And if currency was set to it, vicissitudes (undesirable changes) to gold could cause it increase, which could cause interest rates to climb.

Why can't this be true for employers? Set a "standard" for quality of life and employee's "interest" with the employment relationship would increase.

What should your standard be? How should it look? I don't know. You will have to take a look at this with your teams.

Start with this:

1. Define Relationship

2. Read my definition of Situationship

3. Find out which category your people fall into

4. Determine what percentage is healthy and/or acceptable for your organization

5. Determine what a relationship needs

6. Determine what it takes to move someone from a situationship to a relationship

7. Why not ask them anonymously which of the two they think applies to them?

I read an article where a woman said her fiancé stood her up at the altar – he didn't even make full payment for the wedding venue. And this after dating him for 10 years. They had rehearsals, invited friends and family, and calls to him assured her he was on the way; his Uber was running late.

Chapter 4 – S.T.A.R.

(Stop The Arresting Response)

What is the difference between winning and losing? We should translate this to: What is the distance between winning and losing?

Greater highs see greater lows. It is not uncommon to have feelings of failure when we plan big. What we must do is set aside time to address this fear. This is not the time for determination or motivation. It is time list out our feelings and emotions at this time. Failure to do so means they will come back, and usually at the worst time. This distraction can cause us to miss some important aspect of the work. Imagine, not paying close attention to even the smallest part. This could lead to disaster.

January 28, 1986 the space shuttle Challenger exploded. A failure in a joint caused gas to leak out.

I do not say that someone overlooked this joint, but it should have been caught.

Do you work up to the limit of your ability or your feelings?

This question always gets debate.

Sure, when we are not feeling well, we may struggle to meet expectations – this is natural.

We should make this work specific. Say, you are upset with a new procedure or a decision made by management, and "they" always make things difficult for workers. Will you deliberately not do your job or slow down your production? I have seen unions do this in New York. Silent protest.

Fuzzy Logic – Relatively Yes

This is an extraordinary set of programing used to run electronics. It is more sophisticated than an off or on state. Here, you get varying degrees of "on". Fuzzy Logic is not the typical yes or no found in a binary system. It works with all the possibilities in between – you can open a door up to one inch, two inches, and so on. All the open states can mean something different, but they are all still open. Fuzzy Logic.

Nope. I am not done; let me belabor the point. Some prominent politicians say we should slow down testing for the corona virus, because, the more we test for it, the more people we will find that have it. Sigh.

This is like saying we should slow down academic testing for our children, because we might find a higher number of them that are failing. Again, Fuzzy Logic.

Once you open that door to changing your work ethic it becomes hard to close it – you will always find a reason to keep it open. Here is another look at fuzzy logic that involves me. Years ago, I went to the barber and he asked me if I wanted to "take some off" this area where it is thinning. I was like, "No, don't encourage it."

Okay, we've determined that managing someone's emotions is harder than managing them for work.

I have found that people who operate the extremes of their emotions often produce work that follows the same ebb and flow.

Every Teachable Moment is Not A Teachable Moment

Every teachable moment is not a teachable moment. Well, not for them. That's right, this could be a teachable moment for you. To be more specific, this can be a listening moment, for you. I once had a staff member who seemed to highlight every bad aspect of anything. Even when I could bring resolution that neatly addressed an issue over my pay grade, the staff member would say, "Oh, but why did you have to do this?" or, "Why didn't 'they' do this?" There were times when I would offer: "The workaround was not the goal, it was the means we used to achieve the goal." Now, with this staff member, I found many teachable moments. Not wanting to be overbearing, I decided to be selective with my coaching. Sometimes I just became a sounding board.

As a leader, I have a clear vision of where I want to be. In the case of this staff member, their vision could only see as far as the problem. So, how could I get them to see beyond it? The temptation to interfere and push them forward was great, but I also recognized this as defeating. I seemed to me that the staff member felt like they did not have control over so much going wrong around us. I also recognized that me taking control to help this individual would not help the situation.

The best connections I have made on a one-on-one basis with my team were when we discovered the solution or options together. You see, we cannot get ahead of the situation. Imagine, a person has lived their whole life this way, and you come along in one afternoon, in one conversation, and offer the solution – this is a turn off. We can make people feel shamed or inferior. Leading is not being the smartest person in the room.

Just Let It Go!

Keep in mind if you pass on a teachable moment, you should not bring that moment back. If you do, it will look like you were building a case. And, naturally, their first question would be, "Why didn't you bring this up earlier? Why wait for now?" No matter how important your message is, no matter how right you are, your words will be lost in the "fire".

God gave humanity dominion of the earth. Guess what? Our relationships are in the earth and so is our leadership. Ah, but you say society is unblemished over us and influence is a form of leading. I will take that, but society is not mankind. Society is a group of people with accepted beliefs. What society believes is heavily influenced by the media, popular trends, politics, and religion. This is what your leadership is competing with. Now, we did not consider the team dynamic, individual problems our team members hold, or our own shortcomings. When you have dominion over something, you can name it. God allowed Adam to name animals. Rich and powerful people know this. They name their ships and estates. They even name their problems, like Watergate, Chappaquiddick, and the college admissions scandal. These were situations where the actors acted in the dominion mindset to their detriment. The belief may have been, "I have the ability to do this. I have good reason to this, and so I will do it." The difference is this: leadership will concern itself with what it was given dominion over, which includes the people. Ego will concern itself just with dominion, for benefit of self.

But these are names for domestic issues. The most alarming naming convention is for the United States government. If a DEFCOM 1 declaration is made, nuclear war is evident.

This powerful technology, which can destroy the planet many times over, was invented by our forefathers.

Nuclear power is a form of diplomacy as much as it is a means to an end – a literal end. Our forefathers were of the mind that this threat would keep everyone in check or checkmate; locked in. They understood the danger – a mechanism of peace and war. Generations later, we would

T-Minus Everything and Counting

benefit from their work. But what we see today in our society is a growing abandonment of the other mechanisms they put in place. Let's drop down a few levels to the family unit. There was a time when the matriarch or patriarch was the leader of the family. They taught us valuable lessons and lesions about surviving and thriving. The greatest generation put people on the moon, fought a great war, and did this with less technology than the flagship smartphone you own. Somewhere way back, we all had a generation that was the anchor of the family line. Each subsequent generation became a link in that family line (chain). We learned from the collective knowledge and built on it by adding the next generation (the next link).

Now, popular culture has moved us away from that. Technology, life hacks, and those we associate with (not family relations) have a larger influence over us. I guess this is due in part because the world is smaller, we can connect with more people and exchange more information and resources quicker than past generations, and so there is a smaller dependence of our family. But when we struck out on our own and forgot what our forefathers had established, we broke the chain.

This leaves the current generation trying to anchor a new family line distinctly and succinctly different than the last. The problem with this: No living person can be an anchor. Anchors are planted in the ground. The anchors of our families are the great, great, great ones that are in the ground. Their life lessons and lesions were passed down in the form of legacies – us! We study history in school, fine, but we need to study history at home too.

Shawn Abrams

Whatever happened to Shawn, son of Larry? (My father's name.) What happened to Larry begat Shawn and Shawn begat Aaron? It doesn't make sense to create an entirely new legacy by yourself. Maybe this is why so many countries maintain a monarchy. It seems like a way to root the country and the culture of that country in the traditions and accumulated benefits of their history. But in 2020, to establish, maintain, and project a new legacy in one lifetime is a one-in-a-million feat. Even if this could be done, it would lack the depths to support itself. Some people are chasing anyone's legacy because it looks appealing. Leadership, like fashion, finance, and martial arts extends from a "house". You see, if family and legacy are important, less people will compromise them with their actions.

And now we teach our elders. We must let them know that just because we are related doesn't mean we will follow them. Our elders must be well versed in how to engage the next generation. They must make us feel, think, and act. You don't know how to use the computer; you don't understand kids today. You will see them be spirited away. Don't let me down, House of Abrams! Don't let me become a sad old man because you let my life's work of teaching, coaching, and advocating die with me. If you are a great descendent of mine reading this, I want you to know that I took the time to think about life, you, and your welfare, in your time, my future. Please take a moment to think about life for me, my time, and your history.

I want to define some key terms:

House – the generations. For this lesson, it is the bloodline, but I can also take it to mean raising others with the values, common goals, mindset, pride, and the continuation of these.

Tribe – like-minded people, there need not be any other similarities. Transcends race and culture.

Lack – a shortage. If you can get one you can find another, or you can stretch one to make two.

Tough times – there is lack well beyond that of your peers and/or near peers.

Struggle – tough times, and failure to meet or exceed the accomplishments or success of your parents.

Generational Curse – three or more generations of a family that have the same problem, which is within their power to effect change, but they remain impotent to do so. Unfortunately, no link in the chain will breach. All the links sink down and remain piled up on each other.

Note: In this case there are no learned attitudes of merit to pass along. Not only is there the admission that things are not working, the family is resigned to life as it is. Therefore, a new line must be created as the established one is living dead.

All is not lost. If you feel strongly about this, read on.

Shawn Abrams

Pride 1 - 119

Pride 2 - 122

Pride 3 - 124

Pride 4 - 126

Pride 5 - 128

Pride 6 - 130

Pride 7 - 131

Pride 8 - 133

Pride 9 - 134

Pride 10 - 139

Chapter 3 - This is Beast Mode, too

A twist of fate, moving so slowly it annoys you to watch it unfold. You waited patiently, expectantly to receive what is rightfully yours. Now, trial gives way to trials and you choose to unleash the beast mode.

This chapter is broken into triggers that bring out the beast mode. I decided to call each piece a Pride as each one can take up space (territory) in your life, each is distinct and succinct, yet they can overlap one another, they chase and are chased by the trials of life, and are governed by the cycles of life.

These are the Prides of: "**Beast Mode, Too**"

I introduced "This is Beast Mode" in *The Seven Epaulettes of Leadership*. It had the unintended effect of people I know saying, "I'm in Beast Mode!" when they were upset. The purpose of Beast Mode is to focus your thinking, feelings, and resources into a series of actions to secure your ambitions. It's a reserve inside of you drawn out by situations – it is not anger nor is it revenge.

Pride 1

"One if by land, two if by sea." – Henry Wadsworth Longfellow, Paul Revere

If you founded a country where every man is created equal, and you believe that you should have liberty or death, and you say things like, "don't tread on me", then these ideals apply to everyone who is a citizen of this country.

Likewise, if you say you love someone – you love them in totality. If you lead people, you will also lead them in totality. It would not be fair to lead some and simply manage others. When we enter beast mode, we draw on all that we have – in totality.

During the U.S. Revolution the patriots used unique ways to communicate with one another so as not to be found out or exposed by the British. One such method was to use a signaling system to alert the town that the British were coming either by land or by sea if there were two lanterns on top of the Boston church tower. If the building had one lantern in it, the British would arrive by land. If it had two lanterns, they would arrive by sea.

Beast mode is not a magical state – it's a reckoning, it's an understanding, it's that "wait a minute" moment. Wait a minute, I paid for this, I saved for this, I own it, I studied for it, I entered this relationship with good intentions, I'm not going to be bullied, etc. You can't put me in a bad situation and best me, because I will best the situation.

The Cut of Your Jib

Centuries ago, ships could be identified as friend or foe by the cut of their sail or jib. Makes sense to know what's coming at you while on the high seas. On land, soldiers would use a challenge and password.

The challenge is in the form of a question from an armed challenger like, "who goes there?" to someone encroaching in the area. The person challenged would respond with the correct answer/password, hopefully. The correct password would allow the challenged person access to the area. In beast mode, the challenge(r) is similar in that it presents itself at the most inopportune time. It's whatever is against you or whatever you're up against, but here, the password is different, it represents a pathway to success. The password is not force, power, or a show of strength. It is all the resources you bear; all the experience you possess to achieve your objective. How do you know if you have the right password for that challenge within your beast mode? Well, you will know if you don't have the right password, which means you should not be granted access if you lose more than you've already lost. Example, if you shoot someone in a case of road rage, or you break the law, none of these are a path to success, and so they are not the passwords to the challenge you face – you're just an angry person.

When you squeeze something and there is no space left inside to take the contents, what's inside will come out. Pressure can bring out your beast mode, but it's not comprised of anger. That will run parallel with your beast mode. Whoever you are on the inside will govern what you do when to pressure is on.

In all the world, the best-fought battles were not won with the weapons of war, but with the best strategy. Strategy is the pretext and response to pressure. Okay, we made the distinction between weapons and strategy. Let's now look at the difference between leaders and managers.

Managers see inside the vision, leaders see outside the goal. The manager is a constant reminder of the work, the goal, and authority. The presence of a leader is a constant reminder of our ability to succeed. Additionally, Leaders will inspire the talent and manifest it in others at the most trying times.

The Maintenance of Great Leadership:

Do this by reading leadership articles, taking seminars on leadership, and talking to others who lead effectively. Fuel is not more work, a new assignment, a vacation raise, or promotion. This is important because relationships evolve and change. Your people will face a myriad of problems and we must start out full in order to get them to where they need to be and get ourselves home.

Pride 2

You always bring something back.

Remember Jean Grey? She encountered the Phoenix Force in space, and she brought it back to earth with her. Stay close to me, because I am going to change gears a few times with the next few thoughts.

What Jean Grey brought back had more of an effect on others than it did on her, yet her experience was the foundation for what was to come. The Dark Phoenix.

You see, what you experience is for you, but what you bring back from that experience is what you share with others. The lessons I teach others are what I went through first. It's the Teachers Edition.

You have a choice. You can make the experience a buoy or your anchor event. Tough times will come in like a flood. And rising to the top of adversity requires more effort that sinking down into it. You get to choose. Are you standing your ground or making a point? What did you bring back?

You know, I am one of those people who complained I've come back from a traumatic experience, the same one, multiple times. There is a school of thought that this happens because we didn't learn the lesson from the event the first time, and, as a result, will continue to go through it. I don't doubt this can be true sometimes, but I think other times it is because we didn't teach someone else the lesson. To "go through" and where only you benefit does not help others.

Okay, so, going through the event is a lesson, learning from the event is a lesson, and teaching it to others is a lesson in itself. In the case of baggage, people rarely hold on to it in order to share with others for productive reasons. Although we call it baggage, it's really layers on the person carrying it. Remember, I said you cannot peel off the layers and throw them away. What brought the layer is an experience, a memory – how can you take a memory away? Now we know what we are dealing with. Decide. Are you equipped to surface the person beyond the layers?

I offer you this bit of advice: Don't bring back your ex. We're supposed to learn from the past, not repeat it. I say this because I have seen the Dark Phoenix in past relationships – no thanks; one-on-one, it beats beast mode.

Pride 3

Someone and Always

For someone, there is always a place in yesterday. Always someone willing to suffer for something they don't have. Someone always taking careful aim and always missing the point. Someone always musing about what should have been. Spending too much time thinking about the past leaves us too little time for the present, and not enough time for the future.

It's Happening – Again

Don't spend time preparing for your next relationship by looking in the mirror. Relationships with others begin deep inside of you. Relationships based on your reflection will only last for as long as you can hold that image.

Don't believe me? It's biblical. Recall how God provided Adam with a mate. He put Adam in a deep sleep, and then he took something from inside of him to give back to him.

Let's look at Eve. Her relationship with the serpent was superficial; he was not her mate, just some "random" animal. He offered the promise of gaining something, knowledge, which is something deep inside you, by taking something external to her.

Clue: If you need something external it's not a part of your purpose. It would already be inside of you. Sure, something external can activate this. Eve was not Adam's purpose. His purpose was to tend to the garden. Same for Eve, but they felt possessing the knowledge of good and evil was success.

Success always seems easier, or better. **Clue:** You know you are being beguiled when you are offered some shortcut to something you shouldn't have at that point in your life or at all.

Your purpose is outside of you, but you have what you need to meet it inside of you. If that doesn't make you block your ex's number, I don't know what will.

We're trying to advance through a natural expanse in our lives based on some information some random person told us. That expanse is not just in the literal world – it's inside of us, our thinking. We lack experiences, resources, and a materialized path. No amount of information the random person can offer will naturally fill it. And that's why it's so appealing.

Leadership too begins inside of you. It does not develop externally once you are appointed, elected, or confirmed. Your leadership is uniquely you. You must begin the work of studying the discipline in advance of the position. Your beast mode will be corrupt if you do not invest in yourself. Get some professional development, set aside money, study emotional intelligence, practice relationship building, and learn about successful leaders in your field. A careful review of applicable laws won't hurt either.

Lead your purpose, manage your principles.

Pride 4

You don't want to be the kind of leader or lover that says, "I tried to make you love me, now you're going to fear me!"

Never trust someone that says, "Trust me." These are the words that set you up for failure. The bringer of these words wants to rob you of the process to qualify them for a position in your life.

Relationship Delineation

If you do for me what I do for you, we are friends. If you do for me, but you make me pay for it, I am your customer. If you do for me even when I cannot do for you, we are family and you have earned my loyalty. Herein lies the problem, if you can never do for me, even if I do for you—our relationship is based on hope and patience. But what about the people who have run out of both?

Raising your adult mate in a relationship is as hard as raising money on Facebook for your favorite charity, on your birthday!

More like trying to mature someone inside of a bad relationship is like, well, it's like trying to mature someone inside of a bad relationship. It is not possible to fix people, especially after you accepted them the way they were when you met. People don't change people; leaders don't change people. Situations change people.

No disrespect intended, but we did not detect the shortcomings of this person in the first place, and now in the second place we think we can fix them? If that were possible, we would never have been with them. Don't even get me started on people who have relationship issues with people they are not in a relationship with.

The U.S. and China have a relationship, which can be described as diplomatic to say the least. They are both vying to be the dominant superpower. This is an unequal relationship not because they entered the relationship lacking, it's because there can only be one leader!

The most important export the U.S. has is leadership. My opinion: China is trying to reproduce this leadership. They have become good at acquiring, copying, manufacturing, and repurposing U.S. innovations. But you can't manufacture leadership – not America's leadership anyway. It was born not from studying someone else. It comes from our unique make up, comprised of the frailties of human nature, which we apply the Constitution to address, and those freedoms that we are granted to compound difficulties due to our human nature. Bottom line, we work through problems. Some of the biggest problems we face are our differences. We can filibuster, protest, march, run for office, or just about anything as a form of expression or interest. You can't copy two hundred and forty-four years, or even what you perceive as the best of them.

Change in the moment is for convenience. Change in the present is for the future! – Abrams

Pride 5

Being lonely is okay. I've been lonely many times in my life. Yes, there is a difference between being alone and being lonely, but if you must make the distinction you may be the latter. It's a defensive mechanism, which subconsciously protects but unconsciously withholds you. Loneliness can come in many forms, like achieving success, experiencing failure, and definitely leading others. Loneliness should not rush us into love or unintentionally share the burdens of leadership with those who cannot understand it.

Meet Someone New?

Be prepared to help your "intended" unpack their baggage. Of course, on the first day they look nice and baggage is not visible. Truth is we all have baggage, but some people carry all the stuff they collected from every relationship they ever had. Baggage represents memories and feelings, memories that we refuse to let go. We just hide it from plain view. Do not for one moment think your new potential love will throw it all away for you. You should not feel bad, as this has nothing to do with you. They need help to outgrow these memories with new memories. One thing we can be sure of is if you decide to be with them, they will at some point hold on to your things (memories) as well. We want this to happen. In time, they may let go of overused and outdated things they no longer need to make way for something else. Look at how they packed. Is everything neat or thrown in? Nearly packed memories are intended to stay. This translates into long conversations about what went wrong – the focus is how right they were, baggage comprised of thrown-on memories and misplaced emotions. Whatever you do, don't commit to this person until you see all their baggage. Is what they carry damaged, outdated, or have they clearly have outgrown them? None of these are a love relationship; they are therapeutic at best.

The experience is like writer's block. Why sit there and wait for something to happen? When I get stuck writing, I chronicle my day, look over my plans, reread passages I've completed, or other things that will support the book. Point is, I'm moving forward productively. Before I married, I learned to be comfortable, single, around others. The same is true romance or lack thereof. What can be done now, in advance of that awesome relationship? Well, we should do some awesome things in the meantime. Problems are no different – solutions, peace, and/or God's grace will come.

Pride 6

Beast Mode is not just for getting material stuff back. It can also get you back, from whatever you regretfully lent yourself to.

When your mind is quiet and all the thoughts of the day flood in, this is not to try to address them all. Rest. This is your mind's way of downshifting, purging, releasing stress. To consider these thoughts would force the stress you hold to become useful. Stress can be a reminder, etc.

Using Force to Attain Success

I admit, I do have a way of influencing people, but that's not my normal state of being. I'm not always walking around with quotes or trying to coach random people with their issues. In fact, most of the time, I mind my business. Especially if it is apparent the person I see is projecting their truth and victimizing themselves. What will cause me to coach, say, someone not in my sphere of influence, is circumstance. The situation calls me out. My beast mode surfaces – something must be done; something must be said – it's a morality thing. In this sense, I can use my beast mode to assist others, I would likely use it in support of a joint venture, and I would definitely use it for myself.

A roaring lion will kill no game. – African proverb

Pride 7

You Will Learn

I am your leader, but I may not always be available to encourage you. Maybe I'm tired and I ran out of gas and sat down in the corner and waited for tomorrow to come. I don't need you thinking I'm taking you for granted because I didn't check-in, so I must teach leadership. All the more reason to coach and mentor our direct reports. We need to be in relationship with them. I need to know that if I exit my beast mode, they will surface theirs and, in this case, encourage themselves.

Your failure to teach this and your team's failure to master this is like living paycheck-to-paycheck, which doesn't just limit our living it also limits our thinking.

No, not our ability to think, but our ability to act based on our thinking.

We have extremes, some have so much wealth that they employ others to hunt their food and bring it to them. Others refuse to hunt and ask for food to be brought to them. Only humans live hand-to-mouth. No other animal will take a break from getting food unless they just fed, or they are hibernating.

Predators like lions stalk and chase prey items, because their food has clever ways to escape and unique defense mechanisms to secure their own success. Human beings are not prey items. We are the apex predator on this planet, and it's our job to figure out how to live, how to maintain, and how to grow beyond our means. The "hunt" is a part of life for us. Hunger will drive the hunt. Successful hunters lead and teach others. The best hunters are efficient, but they will invest in better hunting tools like, running shoes, licenses and certifications, designer clothing, ivy-league schools, and social media influencers. The hunt is life – there is success and failure in it. Sometimes predators feel like prey to their problems, but this doesn't change your DNA – your name doesn't become Munson after failure.

Prey items feel sorry for themselves because they're being chased. Predators may miss a meal because they lost the chase, but the only complaining you hear comes from the predator's belly. Silence will fill his mouth for now, but tomorrow will bring beast mode. Every fiber of their being, every step they take, every heightened sense, every bit of information and possible outcome will be focused on one thing – success. Can you do that? Can you put everything you have into everything you want?

Where is your beast mode?

How disrespectful to the hunt and the prey if the kill had to be delivered up to a pride member that did not apply themselves. They refused to hunt. They're not in between hunts, they're not maturing into their beast mode, they're don't have a mechanical or mental disability—they just feel entitled to the kill that they didn't make.

Suggested Reading: *The Seven Epaulettes of Leadership*

Pride 8

Music soothes the savage beast.

Why does "This is Beast Mode, too" have a soundtrack? Well, a part of my writing process includes listening to music. You know how the change in the tempo of a song can influence how you feel? This is how I like to write. I often try to take the reader on an emotional ride or lead them to a period of reflection. The tempo is a constant driving force supporting my thinking, feelings, and actions. For the This is Beast Mode, too soundtrack, I wanted to respect the first offering in my last book, but capture the feeling of reclaiming, restoring, and/or repositioning the reader's feeling toward a difficult situation. Those of you who were trained to perform CPR chest compressions to the tempo of the song "Staying Alive" understand this clearly.

Now, for me, success is my tempo. It is not only the means to an end, but it becomes the pulse of my purpose. It didn't take long to find a musician who could bring my words to life, but it would become another action item to an already long list. Still, I am grateful I took the time to pursue this direction as it helped to motivate me through the last stretch for this project.

Pride 9

I have no qualms about using the resources at my disposal to defend what I have. In fact, I intend to leave any would be "whatever" looking to find God after finding me.

Strike first, get up earlier than "them", launch first. Fear of failure is healthy before you begin, but fear of failing after you start is fatal.

Defensive thinking can only prepare you up to your highest level of thinking.

The age-old question: Which is better offense or defense? You've heard people argue one side or the other – there are good cases for both. I'd like to use the terms Defensive Thinker and Offensive Thinker to represent two different ways of thinking. I know people who can find something negative to say about just about anything, even if something good happened, it was luck or would never happen again.

I don't argue with these people, I only state that what I believe is offensive thinking and I subscribe to it. When I explain this, they usually agree with me – I guess because it seems like it's the most positive way to think. I don't say people who say negative things are negative. I call them Defensive Thinkers and I understand, for them, this is a defensive mechanism.

You know, they were hurt, they lost resources, or they met with some disappoint. But that should be a stray thought left over from that event, not a train of thought for life, because you're putting a barrier between you and success, which are a series of steps leading to purpose. It's the "box" we all try to get out of. We have a brainstorming meeting to figure out how we get out of the "box". Ironically, the same mind that can bring ideas to leave the box can also keep us in it.

You don't need to spend precious years of your life trying to demolish the entire box – that's not purpose, but some people make it theirs. They can spend a lot of time and money for some guru to get them out of something they put themselves into.

If you are like me, you believe in the impossible. We believe logic doesn't always have to follow statistics. Logic is the precursor to endeavor and statistics the result or where it ended. I can follow your logic and I can get a different result. I've heard people tell me, "It won't work – we tried!" True, and it may not work for me, but even if I don't realize the success I want, I still won't fail like someone else did.

Some defensive person will always have something to say, let them talk. That, reader, is why a vision is seen and not heard!

Device A

Centuries ago, castles were good places to hold up. The disadvantage they had was they could be starved out or burned out. In this humble man's opinion, the best defense has a dual role as an offensive weapon. Take the porcupine, its quills form a defensive shield against direct attack, and those same quills can be launched at their attacker. See, his defense does not immobilize or restrict him. You can't move a castle to higher ground or remove it from the line of fire. Offense drives the technological advances of defense.

August 27, 1896 – The 40 Minute War (The shortest war in history)

Opponents: British Empire (Winner) v. Zanzibar Sultanate

The death of Sultan Hamad Bin Thuwaini, Sultan Khalid Bin Barghash seized power. The British demanded that he step down. He did not, he fortified his palace and war ensued. The British attacked from the sea and in approximately forty minutes the war was over. Hundreds of the Sultan's fighters were dead, and he as captured. Sultan Khalid Bin Barghash was not in beast mode. This was just his will and his defensive thinking.

Device B

Let me offer an experience I had with a team I led. I had a heavy schedule at the time and maybe this did not allow me to clearly see what I will share next. Well, I realized the information and even conversation I shared with my team was shared with people outside of my meetings and outside my organization. Now, this wasn't against the law, but it was unethical. I want to say that this person did it for a good reason. Well, their own reason, because if it were a good reason, they would have discussed it with me. In my heart I know this person was conditioned to be this way. This sort of thing was a part of work life for them. This caused me to surface my beast mode, but not to retaliate, not to share what I knew. Remember, Beast Mode does not put you in position to lose more than you already lost.

The first thing I did was resolve the situation within myself with this thought: What would it profit me to confront the person? I see now that some people are defensive thinkers while others are offensive.

Device C

Defensive thinking can only prepare you against your highest level of thinking.

Defensive thinkers play it safe most of the time, they see opportunity as risk, and they will always be behind Abrams, because I am an offensive thinker. I will lead you all the time. And, you should follow me, if for no other reason than curiosity. You never know, it could work, and you stand to benefit if follow me, if you try. The best defense is not in fortifications or defensive thinking. The best defense is to keep your enemy at bay, at home, building defenses. Now, we don't want a defense built for our offense; we need to keep it quiet – it's not a secret if you tell one person. The best secret to hold is the one never told. In the hands of the wrong person your secrets can be as powerful as your leadership, and so it's best not to have any.

In the situation I outlined, my beast mode made me think clearly. If they want to give my information away, I'll start my own rumors.

You still bring causality with defensive thinking. You're making a target out of yourself. Your position/career could be targeted for review because what you are doing is not impactful. Sure, someone could argue that impactful is a subjective word, but we're reading a book about leadership and relationships, and there is expectation for results.

Enter: Rosalind Brewer

An offensive thinker, she made her rocket, and flew it through the proverbial corporate glass ceiling to become The CEO of Sam's Club, and then the COO of Starbucks. She said, "Set a goal that stretches you and work hard to achieve it." Flawless!

Another leader of note who used the Offensive Thinking is Biddy Masson. Born a slave and died a millionaire. Her fortune was made in real estate and the love she showed people. Mason was once herself property and went on to become a property owner. She even founded the first African Methodist Episcopal Church. It took her 10 years to amass two hundred and fifty dollars, which she would use to make her first real estate investment. That's a slow simmering but sustained beast mode.

Pride 10

Not wanting to sound like "blunt force trauma Abrams", but if you go broke spending your last dollar to hurt me, I do not have to go broke spending my last dollar to save you. I would prefer to pray that God would restore to us the way we were when we met. Beast Mode is not about tough love or getting even.

In Beast Mode, I'm not looking to show mercy, because not everyone will learn from the example. They may remember the consequence, but my beast mode is not about teaching, it is about me, getting what I need, getting what I am entitled to, what I lost. It's a recovery mission.

People go to war with each other.

Question: When is the past? **Answer:** right now!

I facilitated a distribution for hundreds of people weekly. You can imagine how much work went into it. Well, one of my volunteers got into an argument with a resident, in front of everyone. I spoke to both parties, and, of course, they had differing opinions of what started the falling out. What I was not prepared for was how long ago the source of their problems had occurred. I learned, after speaking with them separately, that three years ago they had a dispute and because of that they had subsequent incidents.

What I found interesting is while there were many incidents between the two over the years, they both held on to the first one

Shawn Abrams

My lead-in to the conversations was to let them know:

1. I hear you and how you feel is important

2. You feel wronged and the others person should realize this

After listening, I had to remind them why we were gathered on that day.

Right there, in the parking lot, I had to explain that it does not matter who is right or who is wrong or who has the most convincing argument. I cannot referee a matter that transpired three years ago. When you hold on to those kinds of feelings there can be no clear winner. There can only be who has successfully resolved the situation within themselves. What I walked into was their need to validate what they were feeling and what they perceived as the problem. Germans would say, "Schnee von gestern!"

For these conversations, sometimes, we need to provide contrast in lieu of context to mitigate fallout. When new truth comes in, it cannot be accepted because it does not fit the past – it never will, because my reasoning will not make that version/iteration of them, three years ago feel better. Do you see that? Present "me" is fighting for the former me. This happens more often than we know, but I have since learned that in the situation I outlined above, one party was the instigator.

Yes, we realize things may go wrong. That should not be our expectation, but we should be prepared to operate outside of the expectation and professionally or reasonably reposition the person and a situation back into the purpose

You can tell what people seek based on what they lack. Yes, this has a literal meaning on the surface, but when we peer deeper into this, we see that what people lack is what they attack, in you.

Commit to Your Curiosity

At the food distribution, people stop by the table to see what we have. I understand, they want to see if they already have the items we are giving away. But what about the people who, after gaining this knowledge, proceed to ask, "Do you have a (host of other items)?" No, we have only what you see.

Some people stopped by to look for a long time before finally walking away. It looked like they were thinking with their eyes. Would it surprise you if I said that every time I asked someone to sign-in and pick up some food they did this? It shouldn't. I think they looked for a long time just so someone would invite them to take some food. You see, it's different if you give them an invitation. Maybe it's pride, but I don't like waiting for someone to invite me to something good. What do you have to lose?

Okay, that was a good example of committing to your curiosity, let's look at a bad one. August 2, 1990, a coalition of thirty-five countries went to war with Iraq. History tells us Iraq lost the war, but Iraq's leader, Saddam Hussein declared victory. His rationale behind that declaration was simple: He had survived and was still the strongman. Well, he got away with it once, but he went to the well too many times. He was found in what might as well have been a well, a hole in the ground. He would have been better off just looking.

Do you know what happens after land is conquered? You must possess it. Someone must live there and stay there. That's the problem we see playing out with some social unrest.

Some of the most talked about leaders in history thirsted for conquest not leadership. They were already leaders. They made conquest their purpose. And the most ambitious of them would live to see catastrophic failure before their death.

Protesting was a big part of 2020. When you protest you take ground. Do you occupy it? That's not conquering, that's visiting. When the protesting is done people retreat to their homes, and, in time, the collective interest wanes. So physical and literal gains were lost over time. This last case is totally different from the rest, but the protesters looked for a period, and then they went away. As if they were waiting for someone (the authorities) to invite them to change themselves. I don't compare the importance of social/political issue to getting food, but the principle is the same. I think the most effective way to get change is to elect people who support your cause, and to secure the services of lobbyists to speak to elected officials. A hand full of lobbyists would not present as large a front as a street full of protesters, but they know the politicians, they know the laws they want appealed, or need the ones that should be voted on.

So, beast mode is not an angry response to an event. It is a path, which utilizes what you have to get what you want.

Emittam Furorem

The Next 5 Minutes

The Next 5 Minutes is my attempt to restart my videos. It's been some time since I had a consistent number of videos to share. The new shorter format is easier for me to maintain. While the initial offerings will be in direct support of this book, as a whole, they are designed to be a standalone platform. Below, is the inaugural episode, NXT5M:1

Precedent or Protocol

I direct the words in this passage to every American. Our country is called the United States of America because we are a united people. The understanding is that people must have been separate in order to unite them. Granted, we should be the "Uniting" States of America because we are still working on this and likely will remaining doing this. The point is: this is coming together and staying together.

There are some that say Make America Great Again. I say America never stopped being great. This was an idea of freedom that came from a perceived time of oppression. Granted, the framers may not have thought about people that did not look like themselves, but the principle was there for future generations to build on it. I am an African American man who has been racially profiled, and faced other kinds of discrimination, but I will not take a knee during the playing of the national anthem. Partly because I am a veteran, and because I took an oath to defend this country from all enemies, foreign and domestic – there's a lot more to the oath. The solution for America is not to weaken the republic but to build it up. We can't say the entire country is bad because there are problems.

America was founded on great principles and that makes her great from the beginning to forever.

Okay, America is great, but Americans are not doing great things, and that is the problem. I think some people mistake the word great for perfect, or even to your liking. That is what this great experiment is about – it's our differences that make us unique, but our nationality that makes us united. I am not saying we should be color blind, I am saying that we should be blind to color. I would like to see us stitch together the fabric of our society and the different types of people within the same way we stitch together the different colors of our flag. COVID-19 taught us that we can be together but apart. Why can't we teach ourselves that we can be one and we can be many?

That wrong rub is a module. Before you try to jettison the person out of your office—do your best to coach them, and take notes on how their disposition has taught you.

Point: We know we cannot change people, directly, but as leaders we must invite people to change us.

T-Minus Everything and Counting

By change, I mean learn. How can we, as middle-age people, lead younger people based on the preface that we were once their age? When leaders stop leading, they digress to managers. But we all started there. We got our first shot leading and learned some hard lessons, from whom? That's right, our staff!

Now, all these years later, we can't go back to the beginning. As a leader, you will never reach the point where you know it all.

That wrong rub that helped to build you up in a weak areas, provided you allowed yourself to do this, is the preparation you need to not only survive the trip to the next level, but also to thrive once you get there. This will be a new elevation, with new culture, and a different set of norms. And, please don't expect people there to be nicer to you.

Entering the atmosphere of a personal relationship is different because we create it with our person. You would think, "Surely I can withstand something I helped to create, right?" Well, not in every case. I read an article that said the average person dates six people before they find the "one". So, in every one of those other cases when we thought each of those other people were the one, not only were we wrong, but either we or the person we dated could not handle what we created. Maybe the first relationship was infatuation, and subsequent relationships had more complex demands. What we're saying is we can fit together the pieces of what we want but may still struggle to maintain it beyond the beginning. You know how so many people long for that "first love" feeling and person? Well, what if they continue to look for that. "That" was only good for that time. Twenty years later, we've grown and moved on, or should have.

What are we creating in a relationship? A safe space. Something you can share with someone that is oriented on the next level. You want it to be private and special, but at the same time public and worth noticing. You want someone to share life with. Some couples are smart; they build up their relationship by doing things together. But what about the couples that don't build each other up? It would be fair to say that although they are fine as wine, they may not have the ability that you do to withstand the pressures of a relationship. I think we're onto something here. We should also want in this person someone who is willing to learn from us and teach us. Sounds like the Leadership Paradox.

Yes, the person you love will also teach you how to love. Save some time between loving to teach and learn from each other. I don't know what that looks like for each couple, but make some space in the relationship to do this. I can see a lot of well-meaning relationships take off like a rocket, and then fall back down to earth. If in the relationship, we can teach and learn from each other then we won't have to resort to punishing and forgiving. If you have someone, there is nothing wrong with shooting for the stars, for wanting an out-of-this-world relationship, but the work and the fun of it all is in assembling the parts of that rocket.

Chapter 2 – Checkmate

A funny but perhaps true distinction between a diplomat and a politician asserts thus: A "politician" is one who immediately decides to talk for hours about an issue without even thinking while a "diplomat" thinks for hours to decide not to say anything.

- Secretary Perfecto R. Yasay Jr., Department of Foreign Affairs, The Philippines

Quick, give the first reason that come to mind for why you want to be a leader. Now take a few minutes to think about your answer and give your best reason for why you want to be a leader. If it is the same, good. You have reconciled this by giving it thought. And, you are showing off! If your answers are different, you may not have taken the time to consider this. So, do that. It is that important. I will leave you to the business of sorting it out.

Let's move on to the politics of leadership and diplomacy of leadership.

Leadership for politics is concerned with ego, tribe, and power. Leadership for diplomacy is the work of the policy and the details.

Your politics might cloud your leadership – we have seen examples of this in many of the 2020 crises. Diplomacy, on the other hand, will shape your leadership. They are similar, but diplomacy is more of the means and the end than politics is. The most defining difference is politicians require and covet public support. Diplomats work with what is and is not in their purview to bring a balance, not an even balance, but one that will bring opposing sides to rest. Recall my mention of Rosalind Brewer, she could have tried to politic GM's way out of troubled times. Yet, she chose a diplomatic approach, which left room for dignity and fairness to those who suffered. This paved the way to better fortunes and improved reputation for her and GM. Politics takes no prisoners. Politicians will destroy their own countryman for political gain while diplomacy could see an opponent spared for a perceived advantage. I think some leaders get the two mixed up, or they don't know when to move from to the other – these are parallels.

Some nations, technically at war, have parallels that are the only things physically separating them from war. Leaders have parallels too. The first one they would likely face is the one between their politics and diplomacy.

Take Amenhotep III, King of Egypt. His nation was surrounded by peer nations that were cause for concern. His nation abounded in gold, something his neighbors wanted. Yet, he willingly shared his gold in exchange for the princesses of the other nations. A wise strategy as his diplomacy of exchange became as valuable a commodity as gold itself. These marriages helped to strengthen ties other kingdoms, which afforded peace with his neighbors and prosperity for himself.

Diplomacy conceived by will, administered by policy, driven by mistrust, and secured by fear.

Divide and Conquer

Diocletian, Roman Emperor. Split his empire. One east, one west. This was an attempt to more efficiently manage them. Problem: the two sides were not equal, one rich with resources and one not, they spoke different languages, and eventually the western part of the empire fell. The politics between them over food resources and military made no room for diplomacy. You see what happens when you split your people to better manage them?

Where do politics come from? Well, it's usually differences in belief systems.

What drives politics? Usually greed and fear. It doesn't matter what your platform or issue is, it will fall into one of these two categories.

Where do office politics come from? Anything and everything. And, it doesn't matter how old people are or how much education they have. Politics can include but not be limited to: advance careers, prevent being terminated, remove a rival, personality differences, jealousy, etc.

In the office, we want to know what someone's motivation is. It usually stems from something they weren't even hired for. It will be important to review our motivations because motivations lead to expectations. Well, at least they do for me, but I can see how someone's expectations can lead to their motivations.

It would be unfair of us hold someone to an expectation spawned out of our low self-esteem, depressive state, desperation, insecurities, or anything that leaves us feeling less than good.

Rubber and Glue

Emotions are reflected between or bounced off people in relationships. Example: If your person is a runner, they don't love you. If you're chasing them you don't love them. They are running because of some fear and you're chasing them out of fear. Love doesn't make you run or chase.

Question: How do we identify false love?

Answer: These people don't show love when it counts, but they offer love to get credit for it.

Question: How do we identify false leadership?

Answer: It involves growth but not for you.

Love for the people you lead

Example: One of my constituents became upset with me based on a decision I made. She was so upset she hung up the phone. Weeks later, in an unrelated matter she was eligible for a monetary incentive. Other constituents were qualified as well, but she was the only person to follow through, which, in my mind, made her well qualified to receive it. At the time, I recalled the exchange we had, but I put it aside and put her in for the incentive. When she learned what I had done she thanked me for weeks afterwards. I think we agree that she wasn't just thanking me for the incentive; she was also thanking me for not holding a grudge against her. I knew my program was bigger than my feelings. I knew my power wasn't to get back at her – it was to lead her. I believe I led both of us beyond our feelings. As a result, I believe we both grew out of that event. So, leading is teaching. This is also the paradox of leadership. You have the awesome opportunities to learn about leadership by leading others. This person did not leave the door open for a "next" time with me. This doesn't mean I could not be diplomatic with her. The situation needed leadership and I was in the best position to provide that.

Diplomacy also means that even when it's your turn to speak, you don't speak out of turn.

This is a skill. Knowing what is acceptable in social and business formal settings. I take the time discern what is being conveyed by others. I know it can be difficult to lead a group conference call or meeting. And so, I lend myself to the facilitator by trying to be the first person to answer a question. My hope is that it will move others to contribute and move things along. We all know the feeling of "I'm not sure they get it, or they are with me?"

I had a reoccurring meeting with multiple stakeholders. I knew who was on the call, I knew what to talk about, and I held the cards, as in all their questions were directed to me. Well, quite a few of those first meetings felt like an interrogation. My every answer would lead them to ask another question. I thought, "I have to change this. This has to be my meeting." I changed the format. I offered an overview in the form a monologue at the beginning to set the tone and give them something to look forward to later in my presentation. This helped to ease my nerves a bit. What I had to remind myself from time to time was that I wasn't reporting out just on my efforts. I was reporting information about my staff and the community we serve. Now, I can speak with more confidence and authority. I offered thoughtful examples to illustrate my points, my own vulnerabilities, opportunities for me to learn and teach, and I gave them reasons to question me. The last part was huge. By priming them with questions to ask me, I could give my pre-made answer, which, of course, painted me in a positive light.

I think we would all agree that refining our leadership is harder than defining it. If all we intend to do is define, we are locked into that. As complex and dynamic as people are, we can't afford to do this.

Refining our relationships means continuing to work on it. Just because we work at the same place doesn't mean I get to stop working on our relationship. The work is more important than the goal. The relationship I have with my coworker and my relationships with anyone I work with are more important than the work.

The leadership and relationship will keep your team engaged with your vision long after the meeting, and even when you are not in the office.

Communication (S)kills

Kills Soldiers

October 25, 1854, the Crimean War. The Charge of the Light Brigade. This is just a case of bad communication, which got a lot of soldiers killed. The Light Brigade was sent to prevent the Russians from capturing artillery on the battlefield. The miscommunication between the British officers had the Light Brigade engage another artillery battery, which was also prepared for the frontal assault, and they slaughtered the British.

How awesome to know that soldiers will go into battle not thinking of themselves. They think of the collective of their comrades and the order given. Surely, they know that no one solider can accomplish the mission. They also know they can count on every other solider to take the same action to accomplish the same mission.

Kills the Mood

Miscommunication in a relationship can cost you. Imagine, having a nice quiet romantic evening with your spouse, and then this miscommunication occurs. Lights quickly turn on and you see the full color of your spouse's face staring back at you.

Kills Your Reputation

April 20, 2010, BP Oil was responsible for a massive oil spill in the Gulf of Mexico. BP's CEO, Tony Hayward said, "I want my life back!" He no doubt shared his pain, but this was an extremely insensitive statement since eleven people died during the explosion of the oilrig that contributed to the catastrophe. Understandably, the public was outraged by his comment.

I don't doubt this was a good man who made a gaff, but in times of crisis leaders don't focus on themselves. They get the people they lead to focus on them by using inspiring actions and words.

Kills Your Spirit

We all can communicate to ourselves. Some of the internal dialogue we have becomes a belief system. I can't, it won't work – these statements turn into detailed thoughts that stay with us. And we add onto them until we try to support what we believe. Some people think they have diseases they read about until they make themselves sick.

It could be better or could be worse, but who said you had to choose, right now? You can choose what you spend time thinking about. Leaders do this.

Woe unto You, Selfish Leaders!

I often coach new leaders with a caution to the Start Trek leadership. This is where the leaders do all the work. Fighting aliens on the surface of some strange planet? The three most senior officers leave the ship to lead the fight. I know this is a T.V. show and the lead characters are the focus, but that's where that leadership style should end. We should take a good look at why we hold on to work we should let our direct report do. Some of us are afraid these people will replace us. They need to be coached-up to replace us. This is the growth, the need for the future of their careers, and the right-now-today work they do. No matter what your line of business, make your shop one that fosters leadership and relationship building. Add to that, your product of service. We must make the "work" about our team and rally the team around us. If you make the work about the work, you will find yourself trying to rally the team around the work, like calling children back from recess – ahh, man!

We do not have to hold our team at a distance to maintain our position

Woe unto you too, selfish lovers. You cannot expect love, take love, and not give love.

Your destination is on the right.

Division was good early in human development. You remember biology? A single cell divides into two and those two cells divide into four and so on and so on eventually you get a baby that is born. But, unfortunately for humans, we continue to divide ourselves. Only now I'm dividing myself from you based on your religious belief, race, financial status, and for some reason wearing a facemask and division is okay, especially in the US. We have the right to protest things we don't like, but we lost our ability to divide productively. We divide for destructive purposes.

Sometimes division is good because it means multiply. Society division can be good because it means multiply. Dividing is a part of human existence and so is multiplying.

1776, United States of America is born and she has thirteen states. By 1861, she multiplies population and now has thirty-four states. In that same year, United States is broken into two factions – the United States of America and the Confederate States of America, and civil war breaks out. The U.S. is not the only country that had a civil war. There have been more than two hundred civil wars in the world and only three world wars. There is something about proximity that drives humans to divide and multiply. Spend more time fighting our countrymen and fighting other countries

Wikipedia reports that there are approximately one to three million cases of domestic violence each year in the U.S., but it is widely believed this number is under-reported and it's more likely ten million cases. The US is heavily divided over politics, financial standing, race, religion, wearing masks for some reason, and a host of other things. And the home is divided. The point I make is this: It's not uncommon to have division – it's how we started life, how we live life, and how we end lives, as we know most civil wars are won by military victory rather than diplomacy. At some point, you must put down the sword and pick up the pen, but because you won by the sword, you will have to keep it close.

Chapter 1 – Liftoff

The best parts of the apple are the first and the last. The first bite is anticipation of satisfaction, and the last is the satisfaction of that anticipation. -Mary T. Barr, CEO General Motors

An extraordinary leader said, "Don't confuse progress with winning." She's right to say that. So, someone built a rocket. It doesn't mean they are a person of consequence. We have seen Mrs. Barr change the fortunes of GM not by slashing jobs and earning stockholders millions. She accepted ownership for a faulty ignition switch, which led to the loss of lives. After made hard decisions to make things right for the families affected. Her quality and customer service approach brought GM back to success.

I identify with Mary's style of leadership. I know that as a leader, everything I do will lead to an outcome. Knowing this and knowing where I want to go guide my decisions. Or, should I say directions? I need a clear path from where I was to where I currently stand for others to follow. The path ahead is whatever it will be, and I must forge ahead to clear the way.

I told you at the beginning of this book that I have lost a lot, but I am not a loser. I found my purpose in the pain of my problems. Sure, success there was too, but I don't coach success. I coach problems because that's where people get stuck.

We're almost to the end of this book. I have gone on to lead a lot of people. Now that we're about to take off, I thought it fitting to share that, as a youth, I was not considered leadership material. The older boys ostracized me because I was the youngest of the group. I was dismissed as a valuable contributor. This was most evident when we played sports – I was always the last one picked. We all laughed because we knew who would be picked first and, of course, we knew I would be last. There were many young men around who we all saw as leaders, but they didn't teach leadership. In their own way, they exuded it. They would grab someone on their team by the arm or shoulder and tell them what to do. It would seem harsh by an outsider's standards, but we listened. They could get crazy upset and yell at someone for making a mistake, but no one would argue. It wasn't fear that instilled discipline in us, it was the belief that our team captain should be listened to. Following the team captains' orders were as important as winning the game. That was my strength. If I got beat it wasn't because I didn't follow orders. It was because I had a disadvantage against my opponent. When I did get beat and I made eye contact with my captain, the look was disappointment, but I never felt like those feelings were for me; it was a mismatch I couldn't win.

Noted with Thanks

After the some of those games, I would make the highlights. Someone might say, "Shawn, you came close to getting the ball, man. Next summer, you'll be bigger. You'll get it, next summer!" I never got to lead a team back then, but I learned the foundations of being a leader.

These young men didn't know it, but they helped me. Being small and picked last helped me to be okay with feelings of inadequacy. I alone entertained these thoughts myself and encouraged myself. They set the stage in motion for a dynamic leader, someone who would come back to lead him. I don't need him directly, but it ain't over, you haven't heard the last of April.

Review

One of the reviews I received on my last book was that the book seems like a basic introduction to leadership and it was more of a conversation. Now, I thought about it, and initially I was offended and I was like, "Oh, it's not your basic, it could even apply to someone with much experience," and I felt the person was downgrading my effort to just a conversation. But when I really thought about it, I thought this person did capture the essence of the work I cover: a mashup of leadership and relationships, and that they come with complexities of their own, without the extras we sometimes add. My role is to boil down the subject matter to its simplest form to explain it, and when you think about it, you'll find the most effective way to communicate with people is through conversation.

I feel winded, but I can't wait for my second one to come. I have to create it. I have to be my own wind and it's a huge statement. Nothing is really planned on. Coming in, I can boost me or uplift me and I'll think about it. I don't need someone else to do that for me, I'm a leader. I have to do this for myself. I just have to wake up with a smile, a purpose, and a lot of contagious energy. What does that look like? I use the word awesome a lot, "Good morning, awesome team", "Hey, son, how you doing?", "I'm awesome. How are you doing?" And I take the time to slow down and circle back to my people. It happens quite often that I get so caught up with policy procedure, metrics, Helicon tract functions, timelines, entertaining people, priorities, and all these things take me farther and farther away from my base, which is not just a people I serve, but it's the people I work with who help me serve. I have to keep circling back have to check on my circle – even if it's just a call, "Hey, what are you doing right now? I didn't call for a status report for work, I called in a status report for you."

Reset Means Just That

Don't take your problems with you. Each one of us is a center of gravity for problems. And, it seems problems carry their own gravity. This means they too attract problems. You may have heard it said that problems come in threes. Well, some variation of that. Problems, like anything else that comes together, get bigger with each addition. Well, if problems can come together, we may be able to utilize one solution for the set.

It's a Setup: The S&P (Success & Purpose) Mindsets – Detailed

The Success and Purpose mindsets. For your team, winning should not just be about hitting the objective. To do this could wreak havoc on their morale, because not all teams hit their objectives a hundred percent of the time. You need to come up with some other attainable objectives to train and condition them. Remember, I call this success. If they feel success, they can achieve purpose. You are giving them the success mindset in the process. While racking up successes, you are conditioning them for the purpose mindset. They may not be metric-driven or even on a report. This can be something that can be achieved corporately in a time inside of the objective and be in line with the objective.

This is similar to Applied Leadership in that we coach our team, which prepares them for mentoring.

Coaching is building them up where they are, and mentoring brings them to where you are.

Gentle reminder: When coaching we "set up" our people by getting them to feel, think, and act.

In this book, I focus more on the coaching aspect. Mentoring I leave to you, as it should be based on your objectives, their objectives, and everything you learned about them during your coaching time together.

Coaching is not telling people what to do, not directly. It is finding out how they feel about:

- What they are charged with doing
- How they feel about their abilities
- What they understand about leadership
- What they understand about the work they do
- How much coaching they can absorb at any time
- How much coaching you can stand to do at a time
- What they perceive as obstacles to success and purpose
- What you perceive as obstacles to success and purpose

You cannot reach purpose without success, but you can have success (based on your definition) without purpose, and this is where so many people go wrong.

Coaching involves manipulating the ego and the super-ego to make them malleable enough for change.

We'll do this by presenting conditions and situations that cause change in our subject.

Let's create an outline for the work. These are things to keep in mind as we move forward:

- **Vision**: the future, as you would like it to be
- **Plan**: your path to vision
- **Practice**: adversity to your plan
- **Success**: your mindset
- **Purpose**: to realize the future you saw

The ego is a higher function of self, but the id is our animalist side. I know, sounds like it could be beast mode, but no. Beast mode is learned; it is refined – it is a combination of the ego and super-ego.

Domestication

Dog, cats, livestock, etc., these are domesticated animals. Through many generations of breeding, you can domesticate some animals. Selecting desirable traits in an animal pair and mating them should preserve that trait.

Now, let's look at the "animal" side of humans – the id. It holds our basic desires and needs, like eating and mating. Primarily relying on it will make an animal seem wild – we can say the same for humans too. Developing the ego and super-ego will help in domestication.

Let's apply this to our team or significant other. We premised this section with domestication for ease of instruction. Let's remove that word and replace it with the word conditioning. We can achieve change in someone by subjecting them to conditions, which will change their behavior. Subsequent conditions would elicit the corresponding response to maintain that change. After all, if you are teaching people to lead, you need to help them suppress impulsive reactionary behavior.

Same thing with conflict resolution. You are conditioning the person for change over the course of the conversation, not looking to close the situation with every response you give. You're guiding them to what you see and believe they will accept as a reasonable conclusion. For example, if this person did not present an advantageous disposition, punishment or threat does not have to be the condition we offer for change. We can put them in a condition that is "small and low engagement" and reward the successful outcome. This is the campaigning I talk about. It brings about slow a change. If I believe my only recourse it to point out the person's shortcomings, this is viewed as complaining. And complaining brings about long regret. We would likely lose them.

You need a thick skin to withstand friction and atmospheric pressure.

People will rub you the wrong way. If what they do affects you to the point of distraction, it's okay. Let them build up the calluses in that area of your life – believe me, you will need it. I now see the adversity people present to me as modules in my rocket. By themselves, they are not impressive, and you don't recognize the value in them. But they connect to several other parts you need.

Your purpose is not for you, it is for the benefit of others, and so you should not try at every turn to be comfortable. You should not find a great deal of comfort serving others through the auspices of leadership. There will be perks, time for rest and reflection, success along the way, and a quality of life that will afford you the ability to support your work.

Happily, Ever After

Achieving success is like finding someone nice to dance with at a party. Achieving your purpose, well, that's like being able to dance with that nice person outside of the dance floor, and for the rest of your lives, even when the music stops playing. How many couples can still dance together with no music?

Shawn Abrams

Back to Back

Back in the 50's couples, slept in separate beds. Lucy and Ricky were trailblazers back then because they did the very cosmopolitan thing of sleeping in the same bed, on TV no less. Flash forward seventy years, and married couples not only reverted to sleeping in separate beds, they sleep in separate rooms. It's not a judgment—it's an observation. I admire couples who say, "Let's stay married no matter what, and just don't touch my stuff."

Let's get out of bed—we have work to do.

How can we bring the example of the married couples to our communities? It's weird because twenty-five percent of married people sleep in separate beds, but in the same house. Why can't we get our communities to do the same? How can we get people from different walks of life, different races, and politics to stay together, under the roof that is our nation?

There is a movement now to defund the police. I don't agree with this. In fact, I think we need more police. They could benefit from de-escalation training. And we have seen some cases where an officer used deadly force and there was no need to. There is a difference between feeling threatened and feeling scared. Officers need social workers working with them to address mental health emergencies.

The police need to feel like they are a part of the community, not like they are policing the community.

I know there are reports and statistics that show capital crimes like murder, rape, and arson, but I would like other information to be captured and shared with the police. Report community data for the following areas:

- New marriages
- School attendance
- School graduations
- Scholarships
- Number of retirees
- Number of veterans
- New business openings

I want the police to know about positive changes in the community. Imagine, getting statistics about what awful things happened or would likely happen, and you're responding to heartbreaking situations. We need to offset this with good news. We need to bring humanity into the community. The police are responsible for quality of life, and they should know about the life events they contribute to.

How to calculate your payload. If it's people, you're wrong. If it's fear and bad memories, that's not payload – that's drag. Your payload is what you need to support your talent.

Time Travel

We all time travel. We reminisce about fond moments, stew over past disappointments, or take a trip to the future in a dream or a vision. You will find most people fall into one of the two extremes. Some will dream about their past or the future. I don't say we shouldn't indulge in this distraction, but we lose time doing this. Others travel to the future to see a vision of what they want.

All this time travel can serve as a distraction. When we land on a particular place in time we stay for a while. And this affects subsequent trips. Because the "trip" we went on was a bad place, we skip ahead of any good moments, deciding to add on other bad moments. We all mind-trip, but if we cannot shake it off and move away from this thinking, it may be time to talk to someone to help us get through this. There is nothing wrong with getting help when we need it.

I have told many people over the years to make time to celebrate small moments until the big moments come along. We spend too much time working and waiting for something big to happen. We need to busy ourselves with the work along the way. Whatever the outcome you desire, there are phases to it. If your job is to help people get jobs, then you have to refer an amount of people to interview. In order to send people to interview, there are groupings associated with that. We need to set goals along the way. They may not be glamorous goals, they may not be reportable, but they feed into the subsequent goals.

Recycle

At the start, this passage seems considerably basic, but I tell people the work is more important than the goal. Working from goal to goal is like working from paycheck to paycheck. You're going to run out. Sure, you can make it to the next period, but the money you got is already spent. This is what happens with goal hoarding. If we do this, we condition ourselves, and those we lead, to live in this cycle. High one day, paying down and struggling for the remainder cycle.

Cycles are hard to break. They're like the orbit of a heavenly body. They get trapped in the gravity of a larger mass. Imagine: Stuck in this cycle, not liking the day-to-day, waiting for a big payoff, which can be the paycheck or hitting the goal. To get success, you will have to break the gravity of the cycle. Don't let them work for just a paycheck or a goal. Encourage them to celebrate the small stuff as it builds confidence and buys time to get to the big stuff. It keeps them going – now, you can throttle. Once we get into a cycle, we're predictable, and most successful cycles just happen to be hard, boring, or expensive to maintain.

People rarely follow cycles for success, no matter how much they make sense. We follow cycles of comfort and familiarity. Consider the many self-help books that tell us things we already know. The purpose of these books is to break us out of an unproductive cycle and enter a new one.

Have your team recognize that they are in a cycle. Together, you may be able to identify the parts of their cycle. I don't think workers with the same job will have the exact same cycle. Ask them which part(s) they like and dislike. You may be able to reconfigure their cycle based on their work style or strengths and weaknesses. At any rate, the sincere interest in them and what they do is a benefit to your relationship, and this is a logical way to approach a logical problem. I can't stress this enough: Frustration does not spawn success.

Opportunities for Advancement

Not every company has room for advancement. We must find creative ways to address this. What I propose is what a few companies I know do. They have a series of self-testing employees can take on their own time and at their own pace. Tie this into raises and/or promotions. Please do not use it as annual all-staff training – nobody likes that. I don't know what company can produce these tests, but there should be a variety of tests for each position. This could serve to supplement trainings, reinforce the company mission, improve customer service, and can also career advancement prep.

If used as a precursor to promotion, this will help the employee get in the mindset without everyone else knowing. They will take a host of hypotheticals with explanations. All this would be concert with monthly supervision. The supervisor need not have access to the results unless it suggests additional training. Of course, I would want the supervisor to know this, but we assume the supervisor can catch this real-time or within a relatively short amount of time. I want the employee to know that their career does not rest solely in the hands of this one person. The testing can also help the supervisor, as it would point to the team's area(s) of weakness.

1960 President John F. Kennedy signed Executive Order 10924, creating the Peace Corps. Volunteers work in support of foreign governments and organizations that can make use of the help they provide. I like this program as the people who volunteer get training. I'm going somewhere with this.

Some companies have programs where their employees must do some number of hours of community service or volunteer work each year, paid. I want to see smaller companies with few to no room for advancement have their employees rotate through volunteer opportunities where they can learn leadership, organization, resources allocation, team building, and self-discipline, with pay. This will give the employee an opportunity to grow professionally, and what they learn can make them better for the position they hold in the company. Not to mention this will give the employee and immense amount of pride.

The advantage here is that the employee will get a healthy distraction for the valuation of the relationship while securing a benefit for themselves.

Kennedy was the hero that made the program a reality, but the Offensive Thinker who championed the initiative was Walther Reuther, ten years prior.

Shawn Abrams

Re Cycle

Running around a short track, looking for someone to hand a baton to, but no one is there to receive the handoff. Running around a short track, angry and tired.

You could run around a long track and be contented with that because it takes a while to come back to some familiar places – memory lane. Problem is that the places around the track do not change. We change because we get older. We get tired, we pass some other people, and we feel good about ourselves, but we're still on the same track. We run track to practice to win. If life repeats itself in failed relationships and poor decisions, we're on a track.

We run the track because it is a track. It is doable, and it's a track – we can see the area and we can prepare ourselves for the work. It may start out enjoyably, but it's not leading anywhere. For some, it's comforting. Life is not a straight path. The road to success cannot be found on a track.

Let's not fool ourselves with new theories in front of us and history safely behind us. If we are still on a track, we will continue to repeat history.

Nowadays I do my teaching through video and books. Those are mediums of the day. I don't have a paid system for you to subscribe to. If I did and it didn't work for you, I would feel horrible. 2020 took me to some low points in my life. I felt like running away, and every place I approached was alerted to my presence and warned the next place of my arrival. It even felt like my destination moved from its position.

It was extremely hard for me to get this book out this year. This was my impossible, but it's done. I dared to do what I thought was impossible for me. I pray for its success, and I encourage you to achieve your impossible.

If you dare to ascend to higher heights, build your rocket, put the project on a countdown. If you desire to lead, love, and labor to the tune of a next level in your life do it! I'd like to say that you didn't even need this book to do that.

Since I made references to Star Trek, I only thought it fitting to end with this, "Make it so. Engage!"

Roll the Credits

My Band of Gold – these people made this possible my investing in my life:

Motivation and Inspiration

- Jesus Christ

Special Advisor

- Min. Dr. Karen Abrams, my wife, Ma, Pa, and Mama

Editor

- Galadriel Grace - Grace Notes LLC

Spiritual Leadership

- Bishop, Min. Dr. Gabriel Austin & First Lady, Min. Dr. Kathern Austin

Friends – You got my back

- Ron Rodgers
- Deacon Isaac
- Liza Maldonado
- Michele Knox, MBA
- Cheri Glover
- Sonya White

- Pace University – Lubin School of Business

Interview with Abrams

By Yaya Diamond

Dream Chasers Radio

Abrams: This book is about leadership and relationships. We have plenty of leaders today – only, I find that some of our leaders today are more focused on leading their sphere of influence, not a lot of folks outside of that. And they lead people to their agenda, which we might say there is nothing wrong with, but if you are leading someone to an agenda it is a very narrow-minded view of the future. It does not allow for inclusion of others that do not think or see the same way. I think leaders should lead people to vision which is broader. One that is large enough to incorporate or accommodate multiple agendas from different kinds of people. So, I think the book speaks to that. Unfortunately, there is a lot of turmoil and confusion.

Yaya: Okay, I have to ask you, how did you come up with the book cover because I'm loving what's behind you, is that the book cover? No, that is the YouTube series, right?

Abrams: Right, Next 5 Minutes replaces my old series, "Leading in the First Person." They are essentially 5 minutes installments that I call sessions. The first 10 sessions will be season 1.

Yaya: So, how did you come up with the book cover design?

Abrams: I knew I wanted a different book cover, something that stood out. Something like a movie poster. So, the centerpiece is this man on a launchpad. That imagery alone is arresting. You wouldn't expect to see that. Now, I place the man and the launchpad in a valley -it is a low place for him. But he is not concerned with his surroundings, he's looking up in the direction that he wants to go in. We know he is prepared because he's dressed in a suit, but he cannot take off yet. I think that's important to note because so often we get prepared to do something and we think because we're prepared, we're ready to go. No, if you got your driver's license today, you are not ready to go on an open and drive by yourself.

Yaya: I like that idea; I feel like my book cover should be like me being like Wonder Woman or something. Yeah right, I am going to spin around in circles.

So, I heard that you have a soundtrack for one of the tracks. So, what was your thinking behind this because to me all of this is exciting a book and a soundtrack.

Abrams: Well, beat mode is a mindset. It's that wait a minute I am not supposed to be here. This wasn't supposed to happen to me - I need to fix this. And I wrote most of the book in my beast mode. I was so disappointed with how 2020 shaped up. The concept came from a tagline I used in my first book, Leading in the First Person. It grew into, "This is Beast Mode" haven't come up alright so I wrote the book in what I call I was in beast mode so in the first last book I wrote I had a chapter called these mode and it I got a lot feedback for it. This time, I wanted the reader to feel what I was feel when I think beast mode – the written word wasn't enough. I thought music would naturally be a complimentary partner. I found a musician; great guy, he had a few seconds of a track that I knew would be my beast mode. In the first Next 5 Minutes video I outline the scene I gave to the musician to create the track.

Yaya: You know, that's important because I think being a musician myself and being in the music industry, that feeling is of sharing what you feel is the best. can you remember back in the 80's when you first heard that song? What was that song from The Breakfast Club when the guy was holding up the radio? Remember, he was trying to serenade the girl? I was in the movie theater and I was like oh that's so cute he can't sing but he's going to play a song for her.

Okay, so how long did it take you to pull all this stuff together?

Abrams: it took about better part of this year so maybe 7 to 8 months of work. I slowed down in March because of the pandemic. I started the book cover earlier than I normally would to help motivate me to finish. This project was scheduled for release in 2021, but I could not let 2020 pass without my personal response to it.

Yaya: So, who will benefit from reading this book?

Abrams: I would say everyone it does not matter if you're married or single, rich or poor, leading or following, etc.

Yaya: You said in your previous conversations that this book is your answer to the 2020. Can you share that with me, what do you mean by that?

Abrams: 2020 was a surprise, I came into 2020 and released my second book, The Seven Epaulettes of Leadership. I thought this is going to be great. I can promote the book through the rest of the year. And then we are quarantined. I got sick in March too. I am sure I had COVID-19. I am not sick with it anymore, just sick of it. On top of all that, social unrest, and political strife. I thought I do not want to wait until next year, I think I want to surprise 2020. This book and new video series are my contribution my answer or response 2020. People are hurting and they lost someone. There could experience more cases of mental illness as we continue to process this new norm. I want to rally people under a new banner, not a new flag but a new way of thinking, a new mindset. Where leadership is not busy leading their agenda and they care for their people.

Yaya: Will people read your book 100 years from now?

Abrams: I hope not, I wrote this book for these times. I hope future generations take heed to what we lived through and get it right.

Yaya: What's next for Shawn Abrams

Abrams: Everything

About the Author

Shawn Abrams has over 10 years experience in leadership. He has led military teams, corporate teams, and non-profit teams to success. He currently works as a site manager for a community-based organization in New York City. He is also the host of the popular YouTube show *Leading in the First Person*.

Twitter: @abrams360media

Other Books:

Leading in the First Person

The Seven Epaulettes of Leadership

T-Minus Everything and Counting

www.ingramcontent.com/pod-product-compliance
Lightning Source LLC
Chambersburg PA
CBHW072028230526
45466CB00020B/1100